Improve your
Written English

Visit our How To website at www.howto.co.uk

At **www.howto.co.uk** you can engage in conversation with our authors – all of whom have 'been there and done that' in their specialist fields. You can get access to special offers and additional content but most importantly you will be able to engage with, and become a part of, a wide and growing community of people just like yourself.

At **www.howto.co.uk** you'll be able to talk and share tips with people who have similar interests and are facing similar challenges in their lives. People who, just like you, have the desire to change their lives for the better – be it through moving to a new country, starting a new business, growing your own vegetables, or writing a novel.

At **www.howto.co.uk** you'll find the support and encouragement you need to help make your aspirations a reality.

For more information on punctuation and grammar visit www.improveyourpunctuationandgrammar.co.uk

How To Books strives to present authentic, inspiring, practical information in their books. Now, when you buy a title from **How To Books**, you get even more than just words on a page.

Improve your
Written English

Master the essentials of grammar,
punctuation and spelling and write
with greater confidence

MARION FIELD

howtobooks

Published by How To Books Ltd,
Spring Hill House, Spring Hill Road, Begbroke,
Oxford OX5 1RX, United Kingdom.
Tel: (01865) 375794. Fax: (01865) 379162.
info@howtobooks.co.uk
www.howtobooks.co.uk

Second edition 1998
Reprinted with amendments 1999
Third edition 2001
Fourth edition 2003
Reprinted 2005 (twice)
Reprinted 2006
Reprinted 2007
Fifth edition 2009

British Library Cataloguing in Publication Data.
A catalogue record for this book is available from
the British Library.

ISBN: 978 1 84528 331 5

Produced for How To Books by Deer Park Productions, Tavistock
Typeset by Kestrel Data, Exeter
Printed and bound in India

NOTE: The material contained in this book is set out in good
faith for general guidance and no liability can be accepted
for loss or expense incurred as a result of relying in particular
circumstances on statements made in the book. Laws and
regulations are complex and liable to change, and readers should
check the current position with the relevant authorities before
making personal arrangements.

Contents

List of Illustrations

Preface

to the Fifth Edition

Do you have trouble with punctuation? Are you always using commas instead of full stops? Is your spelling weak? Do you have difficulty filling in forms and writing letters? Then this book will help you improve the standard of your written English. It has been written in an easy-to-understand way designed for use by anyone. Whether you are a student, school-leaver, foreign student, an employed or self-employed worker or someone at home, it should prove a valuable reference book.

The format is easy to follow with plenty of examples. At the end of each section there are exercises. Suggested answers are at the back of the book.

Part 1 deals with the basic rules of grammar and punctuation identifying the various punctuation marks and showing how each is used. It also covers the parts of speech and demonstrates their uses. Part 2 shows you how to put Part 1 into practice. There are sections on essay writing, summarising, writing reports and even plotting a short story. There are also chapters on letter writing, filling in forms, writing a CV and applying for a job. The use of e-mail has also been incorporated.

Written in a simple style with frequent headings and easily identifiable revision points, this book should prove invaluable for anyone who needs help in improving his or her written English.

Marion Field

Part One: The Basics

Discovering Grammar

IDENTIFYING NOUNS

Nouns are the names of things, places or people. There are four types of noun: concrete, proper, collective and abstract.

Looking at concrete or common nouns

A **concrete noun** is a physical thing – usually something you can see or touch:

apple	key	queen	umbrella
cat	lake	ranch	volunteer
diary	needle	soldier	watch
garage	orange	tin	zoo

Using proper nouns

A **proper noun** *always* begins with a capital letter. It is the name of a person, a place or an institution:

Alistair	Ben Nevis	Buckingham Palace
Bob	England	The British Museum
Christopher	Guildford	Hampton Court
Dale	River Thames	The Royal Navy

Discovering collective nouns

A **collective noun** refers to a group of objects, animals or people. It is a singular word but most collective nouns can be made plural. Here are a few examples:

singular	*plural*
choir	choirs
flock	flocks
herd	herds
orchestra	orchestras
team	teams

Introducing abstract nouns

An **abstract noun** cannot be seen or touched. It can be a feeling, a state of mind, a quality, an idea, an occasion or a particular time. Here are some examples:

anger	month	peace
beauty	night	pregnancy
darkness	health	summer
happiness	patience	war

Sometimes abstract nouns can be formed from adjectives by adding the suffix '-ness'. There will be more about adjectives in the next chapter.

adjectives	*abstract nouns*
bright	brightness
dark	darkness
kind	kindness
ill	illness
sad	sadness
ugly	ugliness

Other abstract nouns are formed differently. Look at the following examples:

adjectives	*abstract nouns*
high	height

patient	patience
pleasant	pleasure
wide	width
wonderful	wonder

USING CAPITAL LETTERS

Proper nouns and adjectives formed from proper nouns always start with a capital letter. So do the days of the week and the months of the year.

proper nouns	*adjectives*
America	American
Austria	Austrian
Belgium	Belgian
England	English
France	French
Portugal	Portuguese

Writing titles

Capital letters are also used for the titles of people, books, plays, films, magazines:

Mrs Brown	Princess Anne
The Secret Garden	A Tale of Two Cities
A Midsummer Night's Dream	The Cocktail Party
My Fair Lady	Hamlet

Identifying buildings and institutions

Buildings and institutions start with capital letters:

Bristol University	British Museum
Conservative Party	Guildford Cathedral
National Gallery	Surrey County Council

Looking at religious words

The names of religions and their members also start with capitals:

Christianity	Christian
Hinduism	Hindu
Islam	Moslem/Muslim
Judaism	Jew

Sacred books start with a capital:

Bible	Koran	Torah

Religious festivals are also written with a capital:

Christmas	Easter	Eid
Hanukka	Ramadan	

Deciding on subject and object

The main noun or pronoun in the sentence is the **subject** of the sentence. It performs the action. All sentences must contain a subject:

> Fiona was very tired. (The *subject* of the sentence is *Fiona*.)

If there is an object in the sentence, that is also a noun or pronoun. It is usually near the end of the sentence. It has something done to it. A sentence does not have to contain an object:

> The footballer kicked the ball into the net. (The *object* of the sentence is *ball*.)

REPLACING NOUNS WITH PRONOUNS

To avoid the frequent use of the same noun, **pronouns** can be used instead.

Using personal pronouns

Personal pronouns take the place of a noun. They are identified as **1st**, **2nd** and **3rd** persons. They can be used as both subject and object. Look at the following table:

	singular		plural	
	subject	object	subject	object
1st person	I	me	we	us
2nd person	you	you	you	you
3rd person	he, she, it	him, her, it	they	them

It was sunny yesterday. (The *subject* of the sentence is *it*.)

His mother scolded *him*. (The *object* of the sentence is *him*.)

Notice that the 2nd person is the same in both the singular and plural. In the past 'thou' was used as the singular but today 'you' is in general use for both although 'thou' may be heard occasionally in some parts of the country.

Putting pronouns to work

I was born in Yorkshire but spent most of my teenage years in Sussex.

In the above sentence the *1st* 'person' is used because the writer is telling his or her own story. An author writes an 'autobiography' when writing about his or her own life.

Ellen Terry was born in 1847 and became a very famous actress. She acted in many of Shakespeare's plays.

This is written in the *3rd* person. Someone else is writing about Ellen Terry. She is not telling her own story so the personal pronoun used in the second sentence is 'she'. A book written about Ellen Terry by someone else is called a 'biography'.

Writing novels

Novels (books that are fiction although sometimes based on fact) can be written in either the *1st* person where the main character is telling the story, or the *3rd* person where the author tells a story about a set of characters.

Using the 2nd person

The only books written in the 2nd person are instruction books. These include recipe books and 'how to' books:

Take two chicken breasts and, using a little fat, brown them in the frying pan, turning them frequently. Mix the sauce in a saucepan and gently heat it through. When it simmers, pour it over the chicken.

The 'you' in the recipe is 'understood'. 'You' (the 2nd person) are being told what to do. All instruction books, therefore, are written in the 2nd person.

Using possessive pronouns

Possessive pronouns are related to personal pronouns and indicate that something 'belongs'. They replace nouns. They are identified in the following table:

	singular		*plural*	
	personal	*possessive*	*personal*	*possessive*
1st person	I	mine	we	ours
2nd person	you	yours	you	yours
3rd person	he, she, it	his, hers, its	they	theirs

Using demonstrative pronouns

Nouns can also be replaced with **demonstrative pronouns**. These are:

singular	*plural*
this	these
that	those

This is interesting.

That is not right.

These are expensive.

Those look delicious.

Using interrogative pronouns

Interrogative pronouns are used to ask questions. They are used at the start of a question as in the following examples:

<u>Which</u> do you wish to take?

<u>Who</u> is moving into that house?

<u>Whose</u> is that pencil?

> Remember that there *must* be a question mark at the end.

KNOWING THE ARTICLES

There are three **articles**. They are usually placed before nouns and they are : the, a, an.

'The' is the **definite article**. This is placed before a *specific* thing:

> The team cheered its opponents.

'A' and 'an' are **indefinite articles** and are used more generally. 'An' is always used before a vowel:

> He brought a computer.

> There was an epidemic of smallpox in the eighteenth century.

UNDERSTANDING VERBS

A verb is a 'doing' or 'being' word. The 'doing' verbs are easy to identify: to write, to play, to dance, to work, etc.

Looking at the verb 'to be'

There is one 'being' verb. The present and past tenses of the verb 'to be' are shown below.

	present	*past*
1st person	I am	I was
	we are	we were
2nd person	you are	you were
3rd person	he, she, it is	he, she, it was
	they are	they were

Identifying finite verbs

Finite verbs must show **tense**. They can be **past, present** or **future** and are always connected to a noun or pronoun. Look at the following examples:

Yesterday she <u>was</u> very unhappy. (past tense)

He <u>plays</u> the piano very well. (present tense)

Tomorrow I <u>will go</u> to London. (future tense)

> A finite verb can consist of more than one word.
> Each sentence must contain at least one finite verb.

Looking at transitive and intransitive verbs

Transitive verbs are those which take an object:

He <u>trimmed</u> the hedge.

'Hedge' is the object so the verb is transitive.

Intransitive verbs do not take an object:

She <u>dances</u> beautifully.

There is no object so the verb is intransitive.

Some verbs can be used both transitively *and* intransitively.

He <u>wrote</u> a letter. (transitive: 'letter' is the object)

She <u>writes</u> exquisitely. (intransitive: there is no object)

Identifying non-finite verbs

The non-finite verbs are the **infinitive**, the **present participle** and the **past participle**.

The infinitive

The infinitive is the form of the verb that has 'to' before it:

> To run, to dance, to write, to publish, to dine.

If an infinitive is used in a sentence, there must be a finite verb as well. The infinitive cannot stand alone. Look at the following:

> To run in the London Marathon.

This is *not* a sentence because it contains only the infinitive. There is no finite verb. Here is the corrected version.

> He decided to run in the London Marathon.

This *is* a sentence because it contains 'decided', a finite verb. This has a 'person' connected to it and is in the past tense.

Many people consider it incorrect to 'split' an infinitive. This is when a word is placed between the 'to' and the verb:

> It is difficult <u>to</u> accurately <u>assess</u> the data.

The following example is better. The infinitive has not been 'split' by the word 'accurately':

> It is difficult to assess the data accurately.

Using the present participle

The present participle always ends in '-ing'. To form a finite verb, introduce it by using the auxilary verb 'to be'. The past or present tense of this verb is used and the finite verb becomes the **present progressive** or **past progressive** tense. Remember that a finite verb can consist of more than one word.

Ian <u>is helping</u> his mother. (present progressive tense)

I <u>am writing</u> a letter. (present progressive tense)

Julie <u>was doing</u> her homework. (past progressive tense)

They <u>were watching</u> the cricket. (past progressive tense)

Recognising the gerund

The present participle can also be used as a noun and in this case it is called a **gerund**:

<u>Shopping</u> is fun.

The <u>wailing</u> was continuous.

Using the past participle

The past participle is used with the auxiliary verb 'to have'; it then forms a finite verb. Either the present or the past tense of the verb 'to have' can be used. It will depend on the context. Look at the following examples. The past participles are underlined.

She had <u>scratched</u> her arm.

He had <u>passed</u> his examination.

Ken has <u>cooked</u> the dinner.

Chris has <u>written</u> a letter to his mother.

The first three participles in the examples above are the same as the ordinary past tense but 'has' or 'had' have been added. These are regular verbs and the past participle ends in '-ed'. In the last example 'written' is different and can only be used with the verb 'to have'. A number of verbs are irregular, including the following:

infinitive	past tense	past participle
to be	was/were	been
to break	broke	broken
to build	built	built
to do	did	done
to drink	drank	drunk
to drive	drove	driven
to fall	fell	fallen
to feel	felt	felt
to fling	flung	flung
to fly	flew	flown
to leap	leapt	leapt
to run	ran	run
to sleep	slept	slept
to swim	swam	swum
to tear	tore	torn
to win	won	won
to write	wrote	written

When the verb 'to have' is added to the past participle, the finite verb is either the **present perfect** or the **past perfect** tense. This depends on which tense of the verb 'to have' has been used.

present perfect	*past perfect*
I <u>have torn</u> my skirt	He <u>had won</u> the race
She <u>has swum</u> twenty lengths	We <u>had promised</u> to visit him.
They <u>have danced</u> all night.	They <u>had built</u> a new house.

Using the perfect progressive tenses

A continuous action is indicated by the use of the **perfect progressive** tenses. In this case the past participle of the verb 'to be' follows the verb 'to have' which in turn is followed by the present participle of the required verb. The finite verb then consists of three words.

Present perfect progressive

That dog <u>has been barking</u> all night.

She <u>has been crying</u> all day.

Past perfect progressive

He <u>had been playing</u> football

She <u>had been working</u> on the computer.

Making mistakes

The present and past participles are often confused. The *present* participle is always used with the verb 'to be'. The *past* participle is used with the verb 'to have'.

The following sentences are wrong:

I <u>was sat</u> in the front row.

He <u>was stood</u> behind me.

The first suggests that someone picked you up and placed

you in the front row! The second one also suggests that 'he' was moved by someone else. The following are the correct versions:

I <u>was sitting</u> in the front row.

or

I <u>had sat</u> in the front row.

and

He <u>was standing</u> behind me.

or

He <u>had stood</u> behind me.

The present participle is used with the verb 'to be'.
The past participle is used with the verb 'to have'.

Making sense of sentences

Look at the following examples:

<u>To write</u> to his mother. (infinitive)

<u>Running</u> for a train. (present participle)

<u>Swum</u> across the river. (past participle)

These are not sentences as they contain only non-finite verbs. They have no subject and no tense. The following *are* sentences because they contain finite verbs:

He <u>intends</u> to write to his mother.

She <u>is running</u> for a train.

They <u>have swum</u> across the river.

REVISING THE POINTS

◆ Each sentence must contain at least one finite verb.

◆ The finite verb must be linked to the noun or pronoun which is the subject of the sentence.

◆ The present participle can be connected to the verb 'to be' to make a finite verb.

◆ The past participle can be connected to the verb 'to have' to make a finite verb.

◆ Nouns can be replaced by pronouns.

◆ An autobiography is written in the 1st person because the author is telling his or her own story.

◆ A biography is written in the 3rd person. It is the story of someone's life told by another person.

◆ A novel can be written in either the 1st or 3rd person.

◆ An instruction manual always uses the 'understood' 2nd person as it gives instructions to the reader.

PRACTISING WHAT YOU'VE LEARNT

1. Complete the following sentences:

(a) The harassed housewife . . . .

(b) Sarah . . . .

(c) Queen Victoria . . . .

(d) . . . . won the race

(e) His cousin . . . .

(f) He . . . . to play tennis.

(g) The telephone . . . .

(h) He . . . . the computer.

(i) The castle . . . . .a ruin.

(j) The dog . . . . John.

2. In the following passage replace the nouns, if necessary,
   with pronouns:

> Sarah was working in her office. Sarah looked out of the
> window and saw the window cleaner. The windows were
> very dirty. The windows needed cleaning. Sarah asked
> the window cleaner if he had rung the front door bell.
> The window cleaner asked if Sarah wanted her windows
> cleaned. Sarah said she did want the windows cleaned.
> The window cleaner said the garden gate was unlocked.
> Sarah was sure she had locked the garden gate. When
> the window cleaner rang the door bell for the second
> time, Sarah heard the door bell.

See page 161 for suggested answers.

Expanding Your Knowledge

MAKING WORDS 'AGREE'

As well as the pronouns in the previous chapter there are a number of other pronouns. Because some of these are singular and some are plural, the verb is often incorrectly used with singular pronouns. Look at the following examples:

Each of you have been given a pencil.

Each of you has been given a pencil.

The second example is correct. 'Each' is a *singular* pronoun and therefore 'has' should be used as it refers to *one* person or thing. Look at the following examples:

She (one person) has a pencil. (singular)

They (several people) have been given pencils. (plural)

Some other pronouns which are singular and should always be followed by the singular form of the verbs are: everyone, nobody, anything, something:

Everyone comes to the match.

Nobody <u>likes</u> her.

Anything <u>is</u> better than that.

Something <u>has</u> fallen off the desk.

Mistakes are often made with the pronoun 'everyone', which is singular:

Everyone has <u>their</u> own books.
This is incorrect. *Everyone* is singular. 'Their' and 'books' are plural so 'his' or 'her' and 'book' should be used. Following is the correct version.

Everyone has his or her own book.

> Singular pronouns must always agree with the rest
> of the sentence.

Collective nouns, like singular pronouns, must always be followed by the singular form of the verb. Look at the following common mistakes:

The Government <u>are</u> planning a new divorce Bill.

This is incorrect. 'Government' is a *singular* noun. There is *one* Government. The correct version is:

The Government <u>is</u> planning a new divorce Bill.

Most collective nouns can, of course, be made plural by adding an 's'. They are then followed by the plural form of the verb.

The Governments of France and England <u>are</u> both democratic.

INTRODUCING CLAUSES

A **clause** is the section of the sentence containing a noun or pronoun and *one* finite verb. You can have more than one clause in a sentence but they must be linked correctly.

Making use of conjunctions (connectives)

Conjunctions or **connectives** are words that link two parts of the sentence together. If there is more than one finite verb in a sentence, a conjunction is usually necessary to link the clauses. Look at the following example:

She was late for work she missed the train.

The above sentence is incorrect as there are two finite verbs – 'was' and 'missed' – and no punctuation mark or conjunction. A full stop or a semi-colon could be placed after 'train':

She missed the train. She was late for work.

or

She missed the train; she was late for work.

However, the example could be made into one sentence by the use of a conjunction. This would make a better sentence:

She missed the train <u>so</u> she was late for work.

or

She was late for work <u>because</u> she missed the train.

Both 'so' and 'because' are conjunctions and link together the two sections of the sentence. Other conjunctions are: although, when, if, while, as, before, unless, where, after, since, whether, that, or.

Linking clauses

If there is only one clause in a sentence, it is a **main clause**. The clauses can be linked together by using conjunctions which can be placed between them as in the previous examples or they can be put at the beginning of a sentence.

<u>Because</u> she missed the train, she was late for work.

Notice that there is a **comma** after the first clause. If a sentence starts with a conjunction it *must* be followed by *two* clauses and there should be a comma between them. The clause that is introduced by the conjunction is a **dependent clause** because it 'depends' on the main clause.

<u>Although</u> he had been unsuccessful, he was not discouraged.

or

He was not discouraged <u>although</u> he had been unsuccessful.

<u>When</u> her daughter came to stay, she put flowers in the spare room.

or

She put flowers in the spare room <u>when</u> her daughter came to stay.

Look at the following:

This is the coat <u>that</u> I prefer.

When 'that' is used in this way, it can sometimes be omitted without damaging the sentence:

This is the coat I prefer.

'That' is 'understood' and does not need to be included.

Using 'and', 'but' and 'or'

'And', 'but' and 'or' are also conjunctions but they should not usually be used to start a sentence. Their place is *between* clauses and they join together main clauses:

I waited for two hours <u>but</u> she did not come.

He sat at the computer <u>and</u> wrote his article.

'And' can be used at the end of a list of main clauses.

The radio was on, the baby was banging her spoon on the table, Peter was stamping on the floor <u>and</u> Susan was throwing pieces of paper out of the window.

Each main clause is separated from the next by a comma; 'and' precedes the last clause.

'Or' can also be used between two clauses.

> For your birthday, you may have a party or you can visit Alton Towers.

Commas may be used to separate main clauses provided the last clause is preceded by 'and'.

Joining clauses with relative pronouns

Relative pronouns have a similar function to conjunctions. They link dependent clauses to main clauses and usually follow a noun. They are the same words as the interrogative pronouns:

> The house, <u>which</u> had once been beautiful, was now a ruin.

'Which' is a relative pronoun, because it and the dependent clause both follow the subject of the sentence (the house). It is placed in the middle of the main clause and commas are used to separate it. The main clause is: 'The house . . . . was now a ruin'. The dependent cause is '. . . . . had once been beautiful . . . . . .'.

Other relative pronouns are: who, whose, whom, which, that.

'That' can be either a conjunction or a relative pronoun. It depends on how it is used.

The man, <u>who</u> had been bitten by a dog, became very ill.

The boy, <u>whose</u> bike had been stolen, cried.

The player, <u>whom</u> I supported, lost the match.

HANDLING PHRASES

A **phrase** is a group of words that does not contain a finite verb.

Leaping off the bus.

This is a phrase as 'leaping' is the present participle. There is no subject or tense.

<u>Leaping off the bus</u>, Sheila rushed across the road.

'Sheila rushed across the road' is the main clause and it could stand alone but it has been introduced by 'leaping off the bus' which is a phrase. When a phrase starts the sentence, it is followed by a comma as in the example. Phrases add information that is not essential to the sense of the sentence.

Mr Ransome, <u>the retiring headmaster</u>, made a stirring speech at his farewell dinner.

Mr Ransome is described by the phrase 'the retiring head-master' but it is not essential for the sense of the sentence.

COLOURING YOUR WRITING

You now have the basic 'tools' with which to write a variety of sentences. Some types of writing only require the 'basics'. However, other writing needs to be more colourful. You will need to evoke atmosphere, describe vividly and paint a picture with words.

Utilising adjectives

Adjectives are words that describe nouns. They add colour and flesh to your sentence. They must always be related to a noun:

> He bit into the juicy apple.

'Juicy' is an adjective which describes the noun 'apple'. It makes the sentence more vivid.

If there is a list of adjectives before a noun, separate them with a comma:

> You are the most rude, unkind, objectionable person I have ever met.

If the list of adjectives is at the end of the clause, the last one will be preceded by 'and':

> She was elegant, poised, self-confident and beautiful.

Using the participles

Both the present and the past participles can be used as adjectives:

> The crying child ran to its mother. (present participle)

The <u>howling</u> dog kept the family awake. (present participle)

The <u>broken</u> doll lay on the floor. (past participle)

The <u>wounded</u> soldier died in hospital. (past participle)

Make sure that you use the correct participle. The present is used when the subject is doing the action. The past is used when something has been done to the noun. Look at the following:

The <u>bullied</u> schoolboy appeared on television. (past participle)

In the above sentence the schoolboy has been *bullied*. In the following sentence he is the one doing the *bullying*.

The <u>bullying</u> schoolboy appeared on television.

Adjectives are used to enhance nouns.

EMPLOYING ADVERBS

Adverbs describe or modify verbs. They are often formed by adding '. . . ly' to an adjective:

She dances <u>beautifully</u>.

He <u>hastily</u> wrote the letter.

Adverbs can also be used to modify or help other adverbs:

> The doctor arrived <u>very</u> promptly.

'Very' is an adverb modifying the adverb 'promptly'.

They can also modify adjectives:

> The patient is <u>much</u> better today.

'Much' is an *adverb* modifying the *adjective* 'better'.

Other adverbs are: too, more and however.

USING PREPOSITIONS

A **preposition** is a word that 'governs' a noun or pronoun and usually comes before it. It indicates the relation of the noun or pronoun to another word. In the following examples the prepositions are underlined. Notice they are all followed by a noun or pronoun.

> I knew she was <u>at</u> home.
>
> She ran <u>across</u> the road.
>
> The clouds were massing <u>in</u> the sky.
>
> Her book was <u>under</u> the table.
>
> He told me <u>about</u> it.

There has been a tradition that a preposition should be not

be placed at the end of clause or sentence but should always precede the noun or pronoun which it governs.

> Who are you talking to?

should therefore be:

> To whom are you talking?

'To' is the preposition and 'whom' is a relative pronoun. However, as the second example sounds very pompous, this 'rule' is often ignored.

Some other prepositions are: from, above, with, by, of, on, after, for, in, between.

REVISING THE POINTS

◆ Conjunctions or connectives are words that link clauses together.

◆ If a sentence begins with a conjunction, there must be two clauses following it and they must be separated by a comma.

◆ Sentences should not start with 'and' or 'but'.

◆ Relative pronouns are used to introduce a dependent clause in the middle of a main clause.

◆ A phrase is a group of words that does not make sense on its own.

◆ Phrases add extra information to the sentence.

- Adjectives describe nouns and add colour to your writing.

- They can be used singly or in a list.

- They can precede the noun or be placed after the verb, 'to be'.

- Present and past participles can be used as adjectives.

- Adverbs modify or help verbs, adjectives or other adverbs.

- When modifying a verb, they usually end in '. . . ly'.

- Prepositions 'govern' nouns or pronouns.

PRACTISING WHAT YOU'VE LEARNT

1. Correct the following sentences:
   (a) The Government are preparing to discuss the new divorce Bill.
   (b) That class are very noisy today.
   (c) Everyone had done their work.
   (d) The crowd were enthusiastic.

2. Add appropriate conjunctions or relative pronouns to the following passage and set it out in paragraphs.

   . . . it was so cold, Judith decided to play tennis at the club. Then she discovered . . . her tennis racquet, . . . was very old, had a broken string. . . . there was no time to have it mended, she knew she would not be able to play . . . she angrily threw the racquet across the room. It knocked over a china figurine . . . broke in half. She started to cry. . . . the telephone rang, she rushed to answer it . . . it was a wrong number. She picked up the broken ornament. . . . she found some superglue, would she be able to mend it? . . . she broke it, she'd forgotten how much she liked it. . . . she had nothing better to do, she decided to go to the town to buy some glue. . . . she was shopping, she met Dave . . . invited her to a party that evening. She was thrilled . . . she had been feeling very depressed.

3. Add suitable phrases to complete the following sentences:
(a) . . . . , he hurtled into the room.
(b) He broke his leg . . . .
(c) Mr Samson, ... , walked on to the stage.
(d) . . . . , she thought about the events of the day.
(e) . . . . , the child giggled.

See pages 161–2 for suggested answers.

3

Polishing Up Your Punctuation

KNOWING WHEN TO STOP

Writing it incorrectly

My name is Marion Field I'm a freelance writer and I write articles for various magazines I live near several motorways so I can easily drive around the country to do my research the airport is also near me I love travelling and I've visited many different parts of the world this gives me the opportunity to write travel articles I enjoy taking photographs.

There are no **full stops** in the above passage so it would be very difficult to read.

Without full stops, writing would make little sense.

Writing it correctly

The correct version with full stops follows.

My name is Marion Field. I'm a freelance writer and I write articles for various magazines. I live near several motorways so I can easily drive around the country to do my research. The airport is also near me. I love travelling and I've visited many different parts of the world. This gives me the opportunity to write travel articles. I enjoy taking photographs.

Because the passage has now been broken up into sentences, it makes sense. Each statement is complete in itself and the full stop separates it from the next one.

USING COMMAS CORRECTLY

> Beware of using commas instead of full stops.

Look at the following:

She entered the library, it was crowded with people, she didn't know any of them and she wished she'd stayed at home, she felt so lonely.

Here is the corrected version:

She entered the library. It was crowded with people. She didn't know any of them and she wished she'd stayed at home. She felt so lonely.

Commas have a particular role to play but they can *never* take the place of full stops. Full stops are used to separate sentences, each of which should make complete sense on its own. Each one must be constructed properly and end with a full stop.

Breaking up a list

Commas can be used to separate items in a list. In this case the last item must be preceded by 'and':

> Johnny played hockey, soccer, rugby, lacrosse <u>and</u> tennis.

not:

> Johnny played hockey, soccer, rugby, lacrosse, tennis.

Commas can be used to separate a list of main clauses. The last one must also be preceded by 'and'.

> Kit was listening to her Walkman, David was trying to do his homework, Mum was feeding the baby <u>and</u> Dad was reading the paper.

If the 'and' had been missed out and a comma used instead after 'baby', it would have been wrong. Here is the incorrect version:

> Kit was listening to her Walkman, David was trying to do his homework, Mum was feeding the baby, Dad was reading the paper.

Look at the following example:

> The sea was calm, the sun was shining, the beach was empty, Anne felt at peace with the world.

This is wrong because there is a comma after 'empty' instead of 'and'. Here is the correct version.

The sea was calm, the sun was shining, the beach was empty <u>and</u> Anne felt at peace with the world.

Beginning a sentence with a conjunction

If you begin a sentence with a conjunction, use a comma to separate the dependent clause from the main. In the previous sentence 'if' is a conjunction and there is a comma after 'conjunction'.

Here are two more examples with the conjunctions underlined. Notice where the comma is placed:

<u>Because</u> it was raining, we stayed inside.

<u>As</u> the sun set, the sky glowed red.

> There must be *two* clauses following a conjunction at the beginning of the sentence.

Separating groups of words

Commas are also used to separate groups of words which are in the middle of the main sentence as in the following sentence:

Clive, who had just changed schools, found it difficult to adjust to his new surroundings.

'Clive' is the subject of the sentence and 'who had just changed schools' says a little more about him so therefore it is enclosed by commas. It is a dependent clause.

If commas are missed out, the sense of the sentence is sometimes lost or it has to be read twice. Sometimes the meaning can be changed by the placing of the comma. Look at the following:

As mentioned first impressions can be misleading.
The positioning of the comma could change the meaning:

As mentioned, first impressions can be misleading.

As mentioned first, impressions can be misleading.

Using commas before questions

Here is another example of the use of a comma:

I don't like her dress, do you?

A comma is always used before expressions like 'do you?', 'don't you?', 'isn't it?', 'won't you?' These are usually used in dialogue. There will be more about this in the next chapter.

'You will come to the play, won't you?'

'I'd love to. It's by Alan Ayckbourn, isn't it?'

Using commas before names

A comma should also be used when addressing a person by name. This would also be used in dialogue:

'Do be quiet, Sarah.'

'John, where are you?'

Using commas in direct speech

Always use a comma to separate direct speech from the rest of the sentence unless a question mark or an exclamation mark has been used. There will be more about direct speech in the next chapter.

He pleaded, 'Let's go to McDonalds.'

'I can't,' she replied.

MAKING USE OF THE SEMICOLON, THE COLON AND THE DASH

Using the semicolon

The **semicolon** is a useful punctuation mark although it is not used a great deal. It can be used when you don't feel you need a full stop; usually the second statement follows closely on to the first one. Don't use a capital letter after a semi-colon.

It was growing very dark; there was obviously a storm brewing.

The idea of 'a storm' follows closely the 'growing very dark'. A full stop is not necessary but don't be tempted to use a comma. A semicolon can be used to separate groups of statements which follow naturally on from one another:

The storm clouds gathered; the rain started to fall; the thunder rolled; the lightning flashed.

A semicolon can also help to emphasise a statement:

The thieves had done a good job; every drawer and cupboard had been ransacked.

The strength of the second statement would have been weakened if a conjunction had been used instead of a semicolon. Look at the altered sentence:

The thieves had done a good job because every drawer and cupboard had been ransacked.

A semicolon can also be used when you wish to emphasise a contrast as in the following sentence:

Kate may go to the disco; you may not.

'You may not' stands out starkly because it stands alone.

Utilising the colon
A **colon** can be used for two purposes. It can introduce a list of statements as in the following sentence:

There are three good reasons why you got lost: you had no map, it was dark and you have no sense of direction.

Like the semicolon, you need no capital letter after it. It can also be used to show two statements reinforcing each other:

Your punctuation is weak: you must learn when to use full stops.

Using the dash

A **dash** is used for emphasis. What is said between dashes – or after the dash if there is only one – is more emphatic than if there were no dash. If you break your sentence in the middle to make an added point, use a dash before and after it.

> Janice, Elaine, Maureen, Elsie – in fact all the girls – can go on the trip to London.

If the added section is at the end of the sentence, only one dash is needed:

> This is the second time you have not done your English homework – or any of your homework.

REMEMBERING THE QUESTION MARK AND EXCLAMATION MARK

Using the question mark

The **question mark** is obviously placed at the end of a question. *Do* remember to put it there. Students frequently miss it out through carelessness.

> Is it raining?

> You won't go out in the rain, will you?

If you are using direct speech, the question mark takes the place of the comma and is always placed inside the inverted commas.

> 'When is your interview?' asked Lucy.

> 'Are you travelling by train?' queried John.

Using the exclamation mark

The **exclamation mark** should be used rarely or it loses its impact. It should not be used for emphasis; your choice of words should be sufficient. It is used in direct speech – again in place of a comma – when the speaker is exclaiming. There should always be an exclamation mark if the word 'exclaimed' is used:

'I don't believe it!' he exclaimed.

However, the word 'exclaimed' is not always necessary. It can merely be suggested:

'I can't reach it!' she cried.

In this example a comma could have been used but an exclamation mark is more appropriate.

The only other place where an exclamation mark can be used is where there is an element of irony in the statement. The speaker or writer comments with 'tongue in cheek'. What is said is not literally true but is said to make a point:

Jean's Christmas card arrived a year late. It had been on a trip round the world!

REVISING THE POINTS

◆ A full stop should be used to separate statements that are complete in themselves.

◆ Commas should never be used instead of full stops.

◆ Use commas to separate words and groups of words in a list.

◆ Use a comma to separate the clauses if you begin a sentence with a conjunction or to separate groups of words within the main sentence.

◆ Use a comma before expressions like 'isn't it?' and also when addressing someone by name.

◆ Use a comma to separate direct speech from the rest of the sentence.

◆ Use semicolons to separate clauses.

◆ Don't forget to put the question mark after a question.

PRACTISING WHAT YOU'VE LEARNT

Punctuate the following extracts:

1. John was furious he stormed out of the house slamming the door behind him never again would he try to help anyone he'd gone to see Peter to offer financial aid and Peter had angrily thrown his offer back in his face surely he could have shown some gratitude now he would be late for work and he had an early appointment with an important client.

2. The sun shone down from a brilliant blue sky the slight breeze ruffled the long grass the scent of roses was all around and the birds were twittering happily in the trees Emma who had been feeling sad suddenly felt more cheerful the summer had come at last hadn't it while she

wandered down the garden path she thought about the letter she'd received that morning.

3. The team those who were present lined up to meet the new manager they had had a bad season Clive hoped Brian would improve their chance of promotion at the moment the team was a disaster the goalkeeper never saw the ball until it was too late the defence players were too slow and the captain was indecisive.

4. I don't believe it she exclaimed
   Why not he enquired
   Surely it could not be true why hadn't she been told before it wasn't fair why was she always the last to hear anything if she'd been the one going to New York she'd probably only have heard about it after she should have left why had Pat been offered the chance of a lifetime hadn't she worked just as hard.

See pages 162–3 for suggested answers.

4

Paragraphing Your Work

STRUCTURING PARAGRAPHS

Look at the following example:

Stark white and threatening, the letter lay on the brown door mat. I stared at it; my body became rigid. Although I hadn't seen it for years, I'd have recognised my sister's handwriting anywhere. Why was she writing to me now? Forcing my reluctant knees to bend, I stooped down and picked it up. Holding it as carefully as if it contained a time bomb, I carried it to the kitchen and dropped it on the table. Then, turning my back on it, I picked up the kettle with shaking hands and filled it. Hardly aware of what I was doing, I plugged it in and took a mug out of the cupboard. Still in a daze, I made the coffee and took some scalding sips. Then gingerly I picked up the envelope and slit it open. It was a wedding invitation! 'Mr and Mrs Collins' requested 'the pleasure of the company of Miss Cathy Singleton at the wedding of their daughter Lydia . . .' I dropped the card in amaze-ment. Was my niece really old enough to be married? Had my sister at last decided to bury the hatchet or had Lydia forced her to send the invitation? I couldn't believe that I, the black sheep of the family, had actually been invited to the wedding of my estranged sister's daughter.

If you picked up a book and glanced at the page you've just read, you'd probably replace it on the shelf. Sentences have to be grouped together in **paragraphs**, which are indented at the beginning so the page looks more 'reader friendly'.

Deciding on a topic sentence

Paragraphs can vary in length but each paragraph deals with one topic. Within the group of sentences there should usually be a **topic sentence**. This is the main sentence and the content is expanded in the rest of the paragraph.

The positioning of the topic sentence can vary. In the following example the topic sentence, which is underlined, opens the paragraph. It introduces the letter and the following sentences are all related to it. The *first* paragraph is not usually indented.

> Stark white and threatening, the letter lay on the brown door mat. I stared at it; my body became rigid. Although I hadn't seen it for years, I'd have recognised my sister's handwriting anywhere. Why was she writing to me now?

In the next example, which is the second paragraph of the original passage, the opening sentences build up to the final opening of the letter in the last sentence. In this case the topic sentence, underlined, comes last. The following paragraphs are all indented.

> Forcing my reluctant knees to bend, I stooped down and picked it up. Holding it as carefully as if it contained a time bomb, I carried it to the kitchen and dropped it on the table. Then, turning my back on it, I picked up

the kettle with shaking hands and filled it. Hardly aware of what I was doing, I plugged it in and took a mug out of the cupboard. Still in a daze, I made the coffee and took some scalding sips. <u>Then gingerly I picked up the envelope and slit it open.</u>

There follows a short paragraph with the topic sentence underlined. The brevity of the paragraph emphasises Cathy's amazement at the wedding invitation. In the final paragraph the topic sentence is at the end as the narrator's amazement reaches a climax when she gives a reason for her astonishment.

<u>It was a wedding invitation!</u> 'Mr and Mrs Collins' requested 'the pleasure of the company of Miss Cathy Singleton at the wedding of their daughter, Lydia . . . '

I dropped the card in amazement. Was my niece really old enough to be married? Had my sister at last decided to bury the hatchet or had Lydia forced her to send the invitation? <u>I couldn't believe that I, the black sheep of the family, had actually been invited to the wedding of my estranged sister's daughter.</u>

Using single sentence paragraphs

Most paragraphs contain a number of sentences but it is possible to use a one-sentence paragraph for effect. Look at the following example:

He heard the ominous sound of footsteps but suddenly he realised he had a chance. There was a key in the door. Swiftly he turned it in the lock before his captors could reach him. While the door handle rattled, he turned his attention to the window. There was a drainpipe nearby. Opening the window, he stretched out his hand and grasped it. Clambering over the window-sill, he started to slither down. A shout from below startled him.

Losing his grip, he crashed to the ground at the feet of his enemy.

In this case the single sentence of the second paragraph is dramatic and stands out from the rest of the text.

SETTING OUT DIRECT SPEECH

Direct speech is what a character actually says. When writing it, paragraphs are used slightly differently. You can tell at a glance how much direct speech is contained on a page because of the way in which it is set out.

Look at the following passage:

'Cathy's accepted the invitation,' said Ruth.

'Oh good,' replied her husband. 'I hoped she would come.'

Ruth glared at him and snapped, 'I think she's got a cheek. When I think of all the trouble she caused, I can't believe it.'

'You invited her,' retorted Brian, looking amused.

'Only because Lydia wanted her to come.'

Ruth flounced out of the room, slamming the door. She was furious; she had been so sure her sister would refuse the invitation.

Using inverted commas

Notice that the speech itself is enclosed in **inverted commas** and there is always a single punctuation mark *before* they are closed. This is usually a comma unless it is the end of a sentence when it is, of course, a full stop. If a question is asked, a question mark is used. A new paragraph is always started at the beginning of the sentence which contains the speech.

> 'Cathy's accepted the invitation,' said Ruth.
> 'Why did you invite her?' asked Brian.
> 'I invited her because Lydia asked me to.'
> Brian laughed and remarked, 'I'm glad she's coming. I always liked her.'
> Ruth mocked, 'You were taken in by her.'

If a question mark is used, it replaces the comma as in the second sentence. In the fourth paragraph notice that the speech does *not* begin the sentence and there are words *before* the inverted commas are open. The first word of a person's speech always begins with a capital letter.

Interrupting direct speech

Sometimes a character's speech will be interrupted by 'she said' or something similar and in this case a new paragraph is not started because the same person is speaking:

> 'I don't know how you can be so calm,' she said. 'I am very upset.'

There is a full stop after 'said' because the first sentence had been completed. If it had not been completed, the punctuation mark would be a comma and the following speech would start with a small letter instead of a capital letter. Look at the following example:

'I do wish,' he sighed, 'that you wouldn't get so upset.'

There is a comma after 'sighed' and 'that' does not begin with a capital letter.

Returning to the narrative

When the speaker has finished speaking and the story or narrative is resumed, a new paragraph is started:

'You invited her,' retorted Brian.

Ruth flounced out of the room, slamming the door. She was furious; she had been so sure her sister would refuse the invitation.

Quoting correctly

Inverted commas are also used to enclose quotations and titles:

She went to see the film 'Sense and Sensibility'.

'A stitch in time saves nine' is a famous proverb.

The expression 'the mind's eye' comes from Shakespeare's play 'Hamlet'.

Notice that the full stop has been placed *outside* the inverted commas when the quotation or title is at the end of the sentence as it forms part of the sentence.

Avoiding confusion

If a quotation or a title is used by someone who is speaking, use **double inverted commas** for the quotations to avoid confusion:

> 'I think the proverb "Too many cooks spoil the broth" is quite right,' David said crossly.
> 'I wanted to see "The Little Princess" but the last performance was yesterday,' Alison remarked sadly.
> 'Have you seen the film "Babe"?' asked John.
> 'No, but I'm going to see the new "Dr Who",' replied Sarah.

In the last two examples the titles are at the end of the speech so the **quotation marks** are closed first. These are followed by the punctuation mark and finally by the inverted commas which close the speech.

CHANGING TO INDIRECT SPEECH

Indirect speech or reported speech needs no inverted commas as the actual words are not used.

Direct speech:
> 'Cathy's accepted the invitation,' said Ruth.

Indirect speech:
> Ruth said that Cathy had accepted the invitation.

Direct speech:
> 'I want to go to the town,' she said.

Indirect speech:

She said that she wanted to go to the town.

Notice that in both cases the conjunction 'that' has been used. In the second example the first person 'I' has been changed to the third person 'she'. The tense has been changed from the present to the past.

> Indirect speech needs no inverted commas.
> 'That' is added between 'said' and the reporting of the speech.

WRITING A PLAY

When writing a play, inverted commas are not needed because only speech is used. The character's name is put at the side of the page and is followed by a colon. Stage directions for the actors are usually shown in italics or brackets:

RUTH: Cathy's accepted the invitation.
BRIAN: Oh good. I hoped she would come.
RUTH: (Glaring at him) I think she's got a cheek. When I think of all the trouble she caused, I can't believe it.
BRIAN: You invited her.
           (Ruth flounces out of the room, slamming the door.)

REVISING THE POINTS

◆ The start of a paragraph must always be indented.

◆ Paragraphs must deal with only one topic.

- Each paragraph should have a topic sentence whose content is expanded in the rest of the paragraph.

- Short paragraphs may be used for effect.

- Direct speech is always enclosed in inverted commas.

- A new paragraph always starts at the beginning of the sentence in which a character speaks.

- There is always a punctuation mark before the inverted commas are closed.

- A punctuation mark always separates the speech from the person who says it.

- Start a new paragraph when returning to the narrative.

- Use double inverted commas for quotations and titles if contained in dialogue.

- Inverted commas are not needed when reporting speech or writing a play.

PRACTISING WHAT YOU'VE LEARNT

1. Change the following examples of direct speech into indirect speech:
(a) 'Will you come to the dance, Susan?' asked John.
(b) 'I can't go because I'm going to a wedding,' replied Susan.

2. Set out the following dialogue as a play.
'I've got so much to do,' wailed Ruth.
'The wedding's not for ages,' Brian reminded her.

'But there's the food to order, the wedding cake to make and the dresses to buy.'

She started to clear the table. Brian moved to the door.

'I have to go to the office today. I'll be back for dinner,' he announced.

'Wait,' Ruth called. 'I want you to do some shopping for me. I've got a list somewhere.'

3. Punctuate the following passage:

where were you at ten o clock yesterday morning the policeman asked john thought for a moment and then said I was shopping where I cant remember its important john sighed and fidgeted he wished his mother would come in perhaps he should offer the policeman a cup of tea would you like a drink he asked not while im on duty the policeman replied coldly

See pages 163–4 for suggested answers.

Checking Your Spelling

ESTABLISHING THE GROUND RULES

English spelling is not easy to learn. There *are* some rules but often there are many exceptions to the rule. Some spellings and pronunciation appear to be illogical. It is therefore important that certain spellings are *learnt.*

Creating words

There are twenty-six letters in our alphabet. Five are **vowels** and the rest are **consonants.** The **vowels** are A, E, I, O, U. All words have to contain at least one vowel. ('Y' is considered to be a vowel in words like 'rhythm' and 'psychology'). **Consonants** are all the other letters that are not vowels. So that a word can be pronounced easily, vowels are placed between consonants. No more than three consonants can be placed together. Below are two lists. The first contains words with three consecutive consonants and in the second are words with two consecutive consonants. The sets of consonants are separated by vowels:

(a) Christian, chronic, school, scream, splash, through.
(b) add, baggage, commander, flap, grab, occasion.

Forming plurals

To form a plural word an 's' is usually added to a **noun.** But there are some exceptions.

Changing 'y' to 'i'

If a noun ends in 'y', and there is a consonant before it, a plural is formed by changing the 'y' into an 'i' and adding '-es':

berry	–	berries
company	–	companies
lady	–	ladies
nappy	–	nappies

If the 'y' is preceded by another vowel, an 's' only is added:

covey	–	coveys
monkey	–	monkeys
donkey	–	donkeys

Adding 'es' or 's'

If a noun ends in 'o' and a consonant precedes the 'o', '-es' is added to form a plural:

hero	–	heroes
potato	–	potatoes
tomato	–	tomatoes

If there is a vowel before the 'o', an 's' only is added:

patio	–	patios
studio	–	studios
zoo	–	zoos

It would be difficult to add an 's' only to some words because it would be impossible to pronounce them. These are words that end in 'ch', 'sh', 's', 'x' and 'z'. In this case an 'e' has to be added before the 's':

brush	–	brushes
buzz	–	buzzes
church	–	churches
duchess	–	duchesses
fox	–	foxes

Changing the form of a verb

When a **verb** ends in 'y' and it is necessary to change the tense by adding other letters, the 'y' is changed into an 'i' and 'es' or 'ed' is added.

He will <u>marry</u> her tomorrow.

He was <u>married</u> yesterday.

A dog likes to <u>bury</u> his bone.

A dog always <u>buries</u> his bone.

Using 'long' vowels and 'short' vowels

There is often a silent 'e' at the end of the word if the vowel is 'long':

bite, date, dupe, hope, late.

Each of these words consists of one syllable (one unit of sound). If another syllable is added, the 'e' is removed:

bite	–	biting
date	–	dating
hope	–	hoping

If there is no 'e' at the end of a word, the vowel is usually 'short':

> bit, hop, let

If a second syllable is added to these words, the consonant is usually doubled:

bit	–	bitten
hop	–	hopping
let	–	letting

There are, of course, some exceptions. If the 'e' is preceded by a 'g' or a 'c', the 'e' is usually retained. To remove it would produce a 'hard' sound instead of a 'soft' one:

age	–	ageing
marriage	–	marriageable
service	–	serviceable

Adding '-ly' to adjectives

When forming an **adverb** from an **adjective**, 'ly' (not 'ley') is added. If there is a 'y' at the end of the adjective, it must be changed to an 'i':

adjective	*adverb*
beautiful	beautifully
happy	happily
quick	quickly
slow	slowly

If a word ends in 'ic', '-ally' is added to it:

enthusiastic	–	enthusiastically

'i' before 'e' except after 'c'

This rule seems to have been made to be broken. Some words keep to it but others break it. Here are some that follow the rule. All of them are pronounced 'ee' – as in 'seed'.

no 'C' in front	*after 'C'*
grief	ceiling
niece	deceive
piece	receive

Exceptions to this rule are:

either, neighbours, vein, neither, seize, weird

AVOIDING COMMON MISTAKES

Because some words do not follow any rules, there are many words in the English language that are frequently misspelled. These words have to be learnt. Following is a list of the most common:

absence	abysmal	acquaint	acquire
accept	across	address	advertisement
aggravate	already	alleluia	ancient
annual	appearance	archaeology	arrangement
auxiliary	awkward	because	beginning
believe	beautiful	business	character
carcass	centre	ceiling	cemetery
cellar	chameleon	choose	collar
committee	computer	condemn	conscious
daily	deceive	definitely	demonstrative
description	desperate	develop	diarrhoea
difference	dining	disappear	disappoint
discipline	desperate	dissatisfied	doctor

doubt	eerie	eight	eighth
embarrass	empty	encyclopaedia	envelope
exaggerate	exceed	except	exercise
excitement	exhaust	exhibition	existence
familiar	February	fierce	first
foreigner	forty	fortunately	frightening
fulfil	government	glamorous	gradually
grammar	grief	guard	haemorrhage
haemorrhoids	harass	height	honorary
humorous	idea	idle	idol
immediately	independent	island	jewellery
journey	khaki	knowledge	label
laboratory	labyrinth	lacquer	language
league	leisure	liaison	lightning
lonely	lovely	maintenance	massacre
metaphor	miniature	miscellaneous	mischievous
miserably	misspell	museum	necessary
neighbour	neither	niece	ninth
noticeable	occasion	occur	occurred
occurrence	omit	opportunity	opposite
paid	paraffin	parallel	particularly
playwright	possess	precede	precious
preparation	procedure	preferred	privilege
probably	profession	professor	pronunciation
pursue	questionnaire	queue	receipt
receive	recognise	restaurant	rhyme
rhythm	said	schedule	science
scissors	secretary	separate	sergeant
similar	simile	sincerely	skilful
spaghetti	smoky	strength	subtle
succeed	surprise	suppress	temporary
thief	though	tragedy	tried
truly	unnecessary	until	usage
usual	vacuum	vehicle	vigorous
vicious	wavy	Wednesday	watch
weird	woollen	womb	yield

Looking at homophones

Some words that are pronounced in the same way are spelt differently and have different meanings. They are called **homophones**. Here are some examples:

air	gaseous substance	*heir*	successor
aisle	passage between seats	*isle*	land surrounded by water
allowed	permitted	*aloud*	audible
altar	table at end of church	*alter*	change
bare	naked	*bear*	an animal
bark	sound dog makes covering of tree trunk	*barque*	sailing ship
bow	to bend head	*bough*	branch of tree
bread	food made from flour	*bred*	past tense of breed
by	at side of something	*buy*	purchase
		bye	a run in cricket awarded by umpire
caught	past tense of 'catch'	*court*	space enclosed by buildings
cent	monetary unit	*sent*	past tense of 'send'
		scent	perfume
check	sudden stop to inspect	*cheque*	written order to bank to pay money
council	an administrative body	*counsel*	to give advice
current	water or air moving in a particular direction	*currant*	dried fruit
ewe	female sheep	*yew*	a tree
		you	second person pronoun
dear	loved; expensive	*deer*	animal
faint	become unconscious	*feint*	to make a diversionary move
herd	a group of cattle	*heard*	past tense of 'hear'
here	in this place	*hear*	to be aware of sound
hole	a cavity	*whole*	something complete

idle	lazy	*idol*	object of worship
know	to have knowledge	*no*	opposite of yes
passed	past tense of 'pass'	*past*	time gone by
			to pass by
peace	freedom from war	*piece*	a portion
peal	a ring of bells	*peel*	rind of fruit
place	particular area	*plaice*	a fish
poor	opposite of rich	*pore*	tiny opening in skin
		pour	tip liquid out of container
quay	landing place for ships	*key*	implement for locking
rain	water from clouds	*reign*	monarch's rule
		rein	lead for controlling horse
sail	sheet of material on a ship	*sale*	noun from the verb 'to sell'
	to travel on water		
sea	expanse of salt water	*see*	to have sight of
seam	place where two pieces of material are joined	*seem*	to appear to be
sew	stitches made by needle and thread	*sow*	to plant seeds
		so	indicating extent of something
sole	fish	*soul*	spirit
	underneath of foot		
some	a particular group	*sum*	the total
son	male offspring	*sun*	source of light
stake	wooden stave	*steak*	cooked meat
suite	furniture	*sweet*	confectionary dessert
	piece of music		
tail	end of animal	*tale*	story
threw	hurled	*through*	pass into one side and out of the other
tire	to become weary	*tyre*	rubber covering on a wheel

to	in direction of	*too*	as well or excessively
		two	the number
vain	conceited	*vein*	vessel in body for carrying blood
		vane	weathercock
waist	middle part of body	*waste*	rubbish or uncultivated land
weather	atmospheric conditions	*whether*	introduces an alternative

Checking more homophones

'Their', 'there' and 'they're'
'Their' is a possessive adjective. It is placed before the noun to show ownership:

That is <u>their</u> land.

'There' is an adverb of place indicating where something is:

<u>There</u> is the house on stilts.

'They're' is an abbreviation of 'they are'. The 'a' has been replaced with an apostrophe:

<u>They're</u> emigrating to Australia.

'Were', 'where' and 'wear'
'Were' is the past tense of the verb 'to be':

They <u>were</u> very happy to be in England.

'Where' is an adverb of place:

<u>Where</u> is your passport?

'Wear' is the present tense of the verb 'to wear':

The Chelsea Pensioners <u>wear</u> their uniform with pride.

'Whose' or 'who's'
'Whose' is a relative pronoun which is usually linked to a noun:

This is the boy <u>whose</u> father owns the Indian restaurant.

'Who's' is an abbreviation of 'who is':

<u>Who's</u> your favourite football player?

'Your' and 'you're'
'Your' is a possessive adjective and is followed by a noun. It indicates possession:

<u>Your</u> trainers are filthy.

'You're' is an abbreviation for 'you are':

<u>You're</u> not allowed to walk over that field.

Exploring homonyms

Some words have the same spelling but can have different meanings. This will usually depend on the context. The pronunciation can also change. These words are called **homonyms**.

bow (noun)	a tied ribbon or part of a violin	*bow* (verb)	to incline the head
calf	the fleshy part of the leg below the knee	*calf*	a young cow

refuse (noun)	rubbish	*refuse* (verb)	to show obstinacy
row (noun)	a line or an argument	*row* (verb)	to argue angrily to propel a boat using oars
train (noun)	a mode of transport long piece of material attached to the hem of a dress	*train* (verb)	to instruct or teach

USING THE DICTIONARY

Checking your spelling

Use a dictionary frequently to check your spelling. Don't guess the spelling of a word. Look it up. It is helpful to keep a list of words that you have misspelled so you can learn them.

Looking at words

A dictionary not only tells you how to spell a word. It also tells you what part of speech the word is. Sometimes the word appears more than once as it has different meanings and can be used as a different part of speech. Look at the following examples:

land (noun)	(a)	the solid part of the earth
	(b)	a country
land (verb)	(c)	to go ashore or bring a plane down to the ground

fast (verb)	(a)	abstain from eating
fast (noun)	(b)	the act of going without food
fast (adjective)	(c)	firmly attached
fast (adverb)	(d)	quickly

Identifying letters

Letters after the word identify the part of speech:

n. = noun   a. = adjective   adv. = adverb   v. = verb

The verb is often followed by 't' or 'i':

◆ 'v.t.' stands for **verb transitive**. A transitive verb takes an object.

He wrote a letter. (The object of the verb 'wrote' is the noun, 'letter'.)

◆ 'v.i.' stands for **verb intransitive**. This means that the verb does not take an object.

She writes beautifully. (There is no object.)

Many verbs can be used both transitively *and* intransitively – as in the above examples. In this case the verb will be followed by v.i & t.

Exploring derivations

The dictionary will often give the derivation of a word. English is a rich language that owes much to other languages. Some words like 'rendezvous' are obviously French and have been kept in their original forms. Others like 'galley' have been adapted from several languages.

If you have time, browse through a dictionary looking at the derivation of some of our words. It can be a fascinating and rewarding experience.

MAKING USE OF THE THESAURUS

A **thesaurus** can also be very useful. It will help you to find an alternative word (**synonym**) for a word that you have used too much. Words are shown alphabetically and beside each will be a list of words that could replace the word you want to lose. Of course, not all the synonyms will be suitable. It will depend on the context.

Adding to your vocabulary

Using a thesaurus is an excellent way of adding to your vocabulary. It is useful to keep a list of words that you have found so that you can use them again and in this way increase your knowledge. Here is a list of synonyms that could be used instead of the overworked adjective 'nice':

> agreeable, attractive, delicious, delightful, enjoyable, pleasant, pleasing

Roget's Thesaurus

This is the most famous thesaurus; it has two main sections. The second part lists words alphabetically and identifies the parts of speech. After the words are numbers. These refer to the first part where the synonyms for the different parts of speech will be given.

Other thesauri

There are many smaller versions including pocket ones and these can be found in most bookshops.

REVISING THE POINTS

◆ Double the consonant after a short vowel sound when adding more letters.

◆ Learn commonly misspelt words.

◆ Use a dictionary to check spelling and find the meaning of words.

◆ Use a thesaurus to widen your vocabulary.

PRACTISING WHAT YOU'VE LEARNT

1. What is the plural form of the following words?

   lady, company, monkey, tomato, boa, princess, dance

2. Add '-ing' to the following words:

   dine, live, hit, hop, skip, write, mate, mine

3. Form adverbs from the following adjectives:

   happy, joyful, kind, angry, wonderful, clear, quick, careless

4. Correct the following sentences:
   (a) I no you are their.
   (b) I can sea to ships on the see.
   (c) Did you now there house is too be sold?
   (d) Hear is you're packed lunch.
   (e) Their is a whole in your jacket.
   (f) You can go to London two.
   (g) The teacher kept in the hole class.
   (h) The violinist took a bough.

(i) Because of the wind, the bow of the tree broke.

(j) She past threw the crowd.

(k) He through the ball.

(l) Know milk was left today.

5. In the following passage fill in the missing words:

> . . . were no ships on the . . . that morning. She could . . .
> the white foam as the waves crashed on the shore. She
> would . . . when . . . car arrived as it would drive . . . the
> gate. Idly, she . . . a stone into the . . . . The . . . of the
> trees on the cliff . . . swaying in the wind. It was . . . cold
> . . . sit still. Kicking off her sandals, she noticed she had
> . . . holes in her socks. She had intended to . . . her new
> ones. Her hair ribbon had also come undone and crossly
> she tied it in a . . . and stood up, holding her shoes. . . .
> she could . . . the car.

6. What do the following letters stand for?

> n.   v.t.   v.i.   a.   adv.

7. Find synonyms for the underlined words in the following
    passage:

> It was a <u>nice</u> day so the children decided to have a
> picnic. They <u>walked</u> along the cliff path and <u>climbed</u>
> down to the beach. The waves crashed on the shore as
> they ate their <u>pleasant</u> lunch.

See pages 164–5 for suggested answers.

Looking at Apostrophes and Abbreviations

SHOWING POSSESSION

Apostrophes are put at the end of **nouns** when the nouns have something belonging to them.

Making singular nouns possessive

If a noun is singular and it has something belonging to it, add an apostrophe and an 's'. For singular words that show possession the apostrophe is always placed *before* the 's' which has been added:

Karen's handbag was stolen.

Her neighbour's fence was blown down.

The child's ball bounced over the wall.

If the singular noun already ends in an 's', another 's' should still be added:

The princess's bridal gown was made by a well-known couturier.

The thief stole the duchess's jewels.

However, in some cases the extra 's' can be omitted as in the following examples:

James' book was missing.

He damaged his Achilles' tendon.

Making plural nouns possessive

Most nouns add an 's' to make a plural. In this case the apostrophe goes *after* the 's' if it is possessive:

The thundering of the horses' hooves broke the silence.

The ladies' gowns were beautiful.

Some nouns do not add an 's' to become a plural. In this case, if they are possessive, they are treated like singular nouns. The apostrophe is added *after* the word and an 's' is then added. Some of these words are: children, feet, geese, men, mice, sheep, teeth, women.

The children's playground was vandalised.

Kate watched the mice's tails disappearing round the corner.

The men's club room was being redecorated.

The sale of women's coats was postponed.

Using possessive pronouns

When using the possessive form of a pronoun, apostrophes are *not* used when there is an 's' at the end. The **possessive pronouns** are: mine, hers, his, its, ours, yours and theirs.

The blame is <u>mine</u>.

These books are <u>hers</u>. (no apostrophe)

The first prize was <u>his</u>. (no apostrophe)

<u>Theirs</u> was the glory. (no apostrophe)

The success was <u>ours</u>. (no apostrophe)

That house is <u>theirs</u>. (no apostrophe)

Note especially

The cat cleaned its whiskers (no apostrophe).

not

The cat cleaned it's whiskers.

◆ 'Its' possessive does *not* use an apostrophe.

◆ 'It's' is used only when letters are omitted.

◆ 'It's' means 'it is' or 'it has'.

ABBREVIATING WORDS

When writing formally, it is better not to abbreviate. Write the words out in full. However, it is, of course, acceptable to abbreviate when writing dialogue.

An **abbreviation** is when letters are missed out. Sometimes two words are combined into one. An apostrophe is placed where the letter or letters have been omitted:

'cannot' becomes 'can't'

'Do not' becomes 'don't'

'Would not' becomes 'wouldn't'

Note especially

'Could have' becomes 'could've'. *not* 'could <u>of</u>'

'Might have' becomes 'might've'. *not* 'might <u>of</u>'

'Would have' becomes 'would've'. *not* 'would <u>of</u>'

Because of the way the abbreviation sounds, the use of the word 'of' instead of the abbreviation ''ve' is common.

The abbreviation of 'have' is ''ve' *not* 'of'.

Shortening words

When words are shortened, it is usual to put a full stop at the end:

abbreviation	abbr.
adjective	adj.
document	doc.
etcetera	etc.
information	info.
language	lang.

The names of **counties** are shortened in the following way and all need full stops after them:

Berkshire	Berks.
Gloucestershire	Glos.
Hampshire	Hants.

Nottinghamshire	Notts.
Oxfordshire	Oxon.

Other words that are often abbreviated are **titles** but some of these should only be abbreviated if the title is followed by the person's full name. A full stop should be put after the abbreviation if it is used.

Capt. Edward Symes

not

Capt. Symes

Rev. Steven Reynolds

not

Rev. Reynolds

HANDLING CONTRACTIONS

Some words are abbreviated by using the first and last letters only. These are **contractions** of the original word and do not usually need a full stop at the end:

Doctor	Dr
Mister	Mr
Mistress	Mrs
Road	Rd
Saint	St
Street	St

No full stop is needed after a contraction.

USING INITIAL LETTERS

It is becoming increasingly common to describe companies or organisations only by the initial letters of the name of the group. This is now so prevalent that we often forget what the original letters stood for! It is no longer considered necessary to put a full stop after each capital letter. Here are some examples:

AGM	Annual General Meeting
BBC	British Broadcasting Corporation
CPS	Crown Prosecution Service
GCSE	General Certificate of Secondary Education
MP	Member of Parliament
MEP	Member of the European Parliament
RAF	Royal Air Force

LOOKING AT ACRONYMS

Acronyms are words that are formed by the initial letters and we usually say the word rather than the letters:

AIDS	Acquired Immune Deficiency Syndrome
ANZAC	Australian and New Zealand Army Corps
ASH	Action on Smoking and Health
LAMDA	London Academy of Music and Dramatic Art
LASER	Light Amplification by Stimulated Emission of Radiation
NASA	National Aeronautic and Space Administration
NATO	North Atlantic Treaty Organisation
RADA	Royal Academy of Dramatic Art
RADAR	Radio Detection And Ranging
SCUBA	Self-Contained Underwater Breathing Apparatus
SONAR	Sound Navigation And Ranging
UCAS	Universities Colleges Admissions Service

UNESCO	United Nations Educational, Scientific and Cultural Organisation
UNICEF	United Nations Children's Fund
UFO	Unidentified Flying Object
VAT	Value Added Tax

REVISING THE POINTS

◆ The apostrophe is placed before the 's' if the noun is singular.

◆ The apostrophe is placed after the 's' if the noun is plural.

◆ If something 'belongs', add an 's' and put the apostrophe before it if the plural does not end in 's'.

◆ Do not use an apostrophe when using a possessive pronoun.

◆ Remember 'its' possessive does not use an apostrophe.

◆ Put a full stop after shortened or abbreviated words.

◆ Do not put a full stop after contractions, in acronyms or when the initial letters only have been used.

PRACTISING WHAT YOU'VE LEARNT

1. Put apostrophes in the following passage:

Carefully he picked up Johns bundle. It wasnt very heavy. He glanced warily at the caves entrance. It was very dark. The picnic baskets still lay where theyd been thrown. He stepped into the cave and almost fell over a pile of little rubber tubes that looked like mices tails.

Inside there was a boulder of rock. Its smooth surface glistened like gold. Johns hands shook. He wished hed stayed with his brothers. His parents quarrel had upset him and that was why hed run away. In a weeks time they were going on holiday. He wished now that hed stayed at home as hed been told.

2. Correct the following passage where necessary:

The foll doc from Mrs Barker gives info about the lectures to be given by Prof Peter Coombs in Sept and Oct in St Margaret's Church Hall. The Hall is in Church Rd and is situated near the station. Prof Peter Coombs will be accompanied by Dr Martin.

See pages 165–6 for suggested answers.

7

Improving Your Style

RECOGNISING COMMON MISTAKES

Revising punctuation

Punctuation is essential if your work is to make sense.

◆ Do not use commas instead of full stops. If in doubt, put a full stop.

◆ Remember to put a question mark at the end of a question.

Incorrect version

> He was in a hurry, he quickly pushed the newspaper into the rubbish bin, Maria watched him, what was he doing.

Correct version

> He was in a hurry. He quickly pushed the newspaper into the rubbish bin. Maria watched him. What was he doing?

Revising sentence construction

Sentences must make sense. Each sentence must contain at least one subject (**noun** or **pronoun**) and one finite **verb**. If there is more than one finite verb, there are two **clauses** and these should either be separated by a **full stop** or **semi-colon** or linked by a **conjunction**. There are three clauses in the following piece but they are not linked:

> He crept round the corner she followed him she was very suspicious.

There are several ways in which this could be corrected:

> <u>As</u> he crept round the corner, she followed him; she was very suspicious.

> He crept round the corner; she followed him <u>because</u> she was very suspicious.

> <u>As</u> he crept round the corner, she followed him <u>because</u> she was very suspicious.

Checking the correct use of verbs

Always make sure that the **nouns** and the **verbs** 'agree'. If the noun is singular, the verb should also be singular.

> Collective nouns are singular and are followed by the singular form of the verb.

> The government <u>is</u> hoping to win the vote of confidence.

not

> The government <u>are</u> hoping to win the vote of confidence.

Avoiding incorrect pronouns

There is often confusion in the use of the words: 'I' and 'me', 'she' and 'her', 'he' and 'him', 'we' and 'us', 'they' and 'them'.

'I', 'she', 'he', 'we' and 'they' are **personal pronouns** and are usually the **subject** of the sentence. That means they are the instigators of the action in the sentence:

> I like travelling.
>
> She went on holiday.
>
> He has been made redundant.
>
> We have no milk.
>
> They are moving today.

'Me', 'her', 'him', 'us' and 'them' are usually the **objects** of the sentence. That means that something is 'done' to them:

> The ball struck me.
>
> The prize was given to her.
>
> The tree fell on him.
>
> The audience applauded us.
>
> The teacher scolded them.

Confusion often arises when there is a name as well as the pronoun. It is sometimes thought that 'I' sounds better than 'me' but it is actually incorrect:

Tracy and I are going to London.

not

Tracy and me are going to London.

Mrs Jones gave some sweets to John and me.

not

Mrs Jones gave some sweets to John and I.

To check which is correct, it is often useful to remove the proper noun. The following examples are obviously wrong.

Mrs Jones gave some sweets to I.

Me is going to London.

'I', 'he', 'she', 'we' and 'they' are **subjects** and are usually at the beginning of the sentence.

'Me', 'her', 'him', 'us' and 'them' are **objects** and usually follow the **verb**.

However, when a verb is 'understood' at the end of the sentence, it is the **personal pronoun** that is used:

He is taller than I (am).

She was angrier than he (was).

Neither 'am' nor 'was' needs to be included at the end of the sentences. They are both 'understood'. The following examples are therefore incorrect:

He is taller than <u>me</u>.

She was angrier than <u>him</u>.

If the verb was added instead of being 'understood', it would sound quite wrong:

He was taller than <u>me am</u>.

She was angrier than <u>him was</u>.

Revising spelling

◆ Learn the most commonly misspelled words. Revise the list on pages 69–70.

◆ Learn the correct spelling of homophones:

hear	–	here		
their	–	there	–	they're
sea	–	see		
too	–	two	–	to
your	–	you're		

The words 'practise' and 'practice' are often confused and so are 'advise' and 'advice'. 'Practise' and 'advise' are the **verbs** and 'practice' and 'advice' are the **nouns**:

You must <u>practise</u> the piano if you are to improve.

There is a cricket <u>practice</u> in the nets today.

I <u>advise</u> you to behave yourself.

She always refused to take <u>advice</u>.

The **verb** has an 's' before the 'e'. The **noun** has a 'c' before the 'e'.

Avoiding confusion
Other words that are often confused are 'council' and 'counsel', 'compliment' and 'complement', 'principle' and 'principal' and 'stationery' and 'stationary'.

Council/counsel
1. A **council** (*noun*) is an administrative group which has power to make decisions.
   A **councillor** (*noun*) sits on a **council** (*noun*).
2. To **counsel** (*verb*) someone is to help them by listening to them and giving them advice.
   A **counsellor** (*noun*) **counsels** (*verb*) clients.

Compliment/complement
1. A **compliment** (*noun*) is an expression of praise.
   'He paid me a **compliment** today.'
2. To **complement** (*verb*) means to complete the whole.
   'Your scarf **complements** that dress beautifully.'

Principal/principle
1. A **principal** (*noun*) is the head of a college.
   'The **Principal** was very pleased with the students' work.'
2. **Principal** can also be an **adjective** meaning main or chief.
   'The **principal** (*adjective*) boy in the pantomime was played by Joan.'
3. A **principle** (*noun*) is a standard you maintain.
   'In spite of difficulties, she always kept to her **principles** (*noun*).'

Stationery/stationary

1. A **stationer** (*noun*) sells writing paper so **stationery** (*noun*) is writing paper and envelopes.

   I ran out of **stationery** (*noun*) so I had to buy some.

2. **Stationary** (*adjective*) means fixed in one place.

   The train was **stationary** (*adjective*) at the platform.

Looking at common mistakes

A mistake that is frequently heard is the following:

> He is very different <u>to</u> his brother.

This is wrong. It should be:

> He is very different <u>from</u> his brother.

If you **differ**, you move away **from**.
If you are **similar**, you are similar **to**.

Checking apostrophes and abbreviations

◆ Do not put an apostrophe every time there is a plural word ending in 's'.

◆ The abbreviation of 'could have' is 'could've' *not* 'could of'.

◆ Do not put a full stop after a contraction:

Doctor	–	Dr
Mister	–	Mr

AVOIDING UNNECESSARY REPETITION

◆ Remember that **nouns** do not usually need to be repeated within the same sentence.

◆ Replace them with **pronouns**:

He tried on his new boots. The boots were too tight.

This should be:

He tried on his new boots. They were too tight.

Rejecting tautologies

A tautology is where the same thing is said twice over in different ways, for example:

The last chapter will be at the end of the book.

The people applauded by clapping their hands.

These two sentences are repetitious. 'The last chapter' will obviously be at the end so it is not necessary to say so. 'Applause' is usually shown by clapping so 'by clapping their hands' is unnecessary.

Varying the sentence

If sentences frequently begin with the same word, the word becomes monotonous. Avoid the temptation to start consecutive sentences in the same way.

She cautiously opened the door. She saw who stood on the doorstep so she hurriedly closed it. She ran back to the dining room. She started to cry. She was distraught.

These five sentences all start with 'she' so the passage does not flow. Is the following example better?

> Cautiously opening the door, Tina saw who stood on the doorstep so she hurriedly closed it. Running back to the dining room, the child started to cry. She was distraught.

Sentences 3 and 4 have been combined and only the last sentence starts with 'she' while two of the pronouns have been replaced with nouns. The writing is much 'tighter'.

MAKING COMPARISONS

When using adjectives to compare two things or people '-er' is usually added to the base word. This is known as the comparative. The base word is 'positive'.

positive	comparative
big	bigger
happy	happier
slow	slower
tall	taller

She is <u>taller</u> than I am.

He is <u>slower</u> than she is.

When more than two things or people are involved, '-est' is added to the adjective. This is known as the superlative:

positive	comparative	superlative
big	bigger	biggest

happy	happier	happiest
slow	slower	slowest
tall	taller	tallest

Adrian is the <u>biggest</u> of all the boys.

Mary is the <u>tallest</u> of the four girls.

Some words are so constructed that to add the suffix '-er' or '- est' would produce clumsy words. In this case 'more' and 'most' are put before the adjective instead:

beautiful	more beautiful	most beautiful
excitable	more excitable	most excitable
intelligent	more intelligent	most intelligent
irritable	more irritable	most irritable

Joanne was the most beautiful girl Frank had ever seen.

Gail was the most intelligent student in the class.

> 'More' and 'most' cannot be used if '-er' or '-est' have been used.

'Bad', 'good' and 'little' do not follow the rules and have their own words for comparison:

bad	worse	worst
good	better	best
little	less	least

The patient is <u>worse</u> today.

Clive is the <u>best</u> pupil I have ever taught.

That is the <u>least</u> of my worries.

ELIMINATING JARGON

Looking at the origin

The word 'jargon' is derived from a Middle English word meaning 'meaningless chatter'. The derivation suggests a very good reason why jargon should be avoided. Anyone who is a member of a group uses jargon that is intelligible only to other members of the same group. Lawyers have their own jargon and so do politicians, schoolteachers and nurses.

Today we are bombarded with words ending in 'ise'. Privatise, normalise, prioritise, nationalise are all words that are now embedded in our language. But they are jargon and should be avoided, as should all forms of jargon. Use words and expressions that will be easily understood by anyone who reads your work. Strive always for originality and simplicity in your writing. Look at the following example:

> The local council is producing a programme to normalise the work experience schedule of students in its employ. Any input from department heads to finalise this should be submitted by the due date.

It's full of jargon. But it is an internal note so should be understood by its readers. The following example is very pompous:

> Louis had fed in the appropriate information before finalising his entry. Now he hurtled along the race track hoping to maximise his potential.

Here is the simplified version:

> Louis had given all the appropriate information before entering the race. Now he hurtled along the track, hoping to win.

Avoid jargon. Aim for simplicity.

STIMULATING YOUR IMAGINATION

Avoiding clichés

Clichés are phrases that are heard over and over again. We all use them and they are often very apt. Of course, they were original when they were said for the first time. Many of their origins have been lost but a number owe their existence to the Bible and Shakespeare. The following expressions are probably familiar although the original words have sometimes been changed slightly:

> All that glistens (glisters) is not gold. (*Merchant of Venice*, Shakespeare)
>
> My mind's eye. (*Hamlet*, Shakespeare)
>
> Don't hide your light under a bushel. (The Bible)

Here are some more common examples:

> He stopped dead in his tracks.
>
> She went as white as a sheet.
>
> He ran like the wind.

Creating similes

The last two examples were **similes**. These are comparisons between two things using the words 'like' or 'as', Many clichés are similes and they are often very vivid. However, they are not original and you should avoid them. It is much better to create your own 'images' so that your reader will be struck by the originality of your writing. If you want to create a simile using a colour, try to think of something unusual which is that colour. The face of someone who is seasick might be said to be 'as green as grass' but 'as green as the mould at the bottom of an unwashed milk bottle' is far more original if not very pleasant.

'My legs felt like jelly' is not original although it is apt. The following suggests the same feeling but is more vivid because it is original:

> My legs felt like spaghetti that had just been dipped into boiling water.

Producing metaphors

Metaphors are also comparisons but they are 'implied' and do not use 'like' or 'as'. We use metaphorical language a great deal in everyday speech. It is language that is not literally true but cannot be classified as a lie as everyone knows what is meant. Look at the following examples:

> I'm starving.

> He says he's freezing.

> She's dying of thirst.

All of the above examples are clichés and all are metaphors. The language is metaphorical – not literally true. If it were true, all three characters would be dead and we know that is not what is meant.

> The moon is a silver ball in the dark sky.

This is a metaphor but if 'like' is added, it becomes a simile:

> The moon is <u>like</u> a silver ball in the dark sky.

Metaphors and **similes** both add interest to your writing but they should be used sparingly.

Personifying inanimate objects

To **personify** means to give an inanimate object human characteristics. Look at the following examples:

> The sun walked across the sky in her golden shoes.
> The table groaned under the weight of the food.

Both use **personification**. The sun 'walks' and wears 'golden shoes'. The table 'groans'. They are also metaphors as they are not literally true.

The use of the **figures of speech** we have just discussed, is common in prose writing and adds to the interest. **Prose** is written and spoken language that does not have a regular beat or rhyme as some poetry does.

Economising on words

Good writing is simple and easy to understand. Unnecessary words should be eliminated. If one word can replace four, use it. Look at the following 'wordy' example:

> All of a sudden, he ran quickly to the computer. He knew it was absolutely essential to eliminate completely his very unique work which, although extremely excellent, could put him in bad danger. In the event that his enemies found and discovered what he had done, he would try to give advance warning of the catastrophic disaster that would follow.

A number of the words and phrases in this example are **tautologies**. They repeat what has already been said and are quite unnecessary. 'Unique' and 'excellent' cannot be qualified. They stand alone. Other expressions could be shortened to make the work flow. The passage could be tightened up by the removal of many extra words. Why use 'all of a sudden' when 'suddenly' will do? 'Eliminate' and 'essential' do nct need to be qualified. 'Absolutely', 'completely', 'very', and 'extremely' therefore should be deleted. 'Bad danger', 'advance warning' and 'catastrophic disaster' are also wrong. 'Danger' *is* 'bad', a 'warning' always refers to the future and a 'disaster' *is* 'catastrophic'. Look at the revised version:

> Suddenly, he rushed to the computer. He knew it was essential to eliminate his unique work, which, although excellent, could put him in danger. If his enemies discovered what he had done, he would try to

give warning to the world of the disaster that would follow.

Making use of the active and passive voice

The **active voice** is more positive than the **passive voice**. In the **active voice** a subject does something. In the **passive voice** something is done to him.

Active voice

The father struck his son.

The teacher gave the class a detention.

Passive voice

The son was struck by his father.

The class was given a detention by the teacher.

In the second version there are two extra words; the first sentences have more vigour.

Negatives

Using positive statements instead of negative ones also economises on words.

For example:

He did not remember his wife's birthday.

Clare was not present in the afternoon.

would be better as the following:

He forgot his wife's birthday.

Clare was absent in the afternoon.

Avoid double negatives which make a positive:

There isn't no one there.

I haven't got no lunch.

The 'not' and the 'no' cancel each other out and therefore the first example means there *is* someone there and the second means I *have* got some lunch.

There is a choice of two correct versions. Only *one* negative should be used if the sense is to be kept:

There isn't anyone there.

or

There is no one there.

I haven't got any lunch.

or

I have no lunch.

Avoid double negatives.

CHECKING YOUR WORK

Always check your work to make sure that it makes sense. Avoid vagueness and expressions which add nothing to your sentence. Some expressions to be avoided are: 'to tell you the truth', 'in fact', 'actually'.

> Avoid clichés, jargon, tautologies and unnecessary words.

Make sure your **phrases** and **clauses** are in the right order so there is no confusion:

She put the letter on the desk which had been opened.

In the above, 'which had been opened' refers to the letter not the desk so it should follow 'letter'. The following is the correct version:

She put the letter, which had been opened, on the desk.

Here's another example:

The knife was very sharp which he used.

The correct version is:

The knife, which he used, was very sharp.

Aim to develop your own individual style of writing. Read widely so you can appreciate others' writing but do not copy them. Always check your work carefully to make sure your sentences make sense, are well-constructed and do not contain any careless mistakes.

Avoid repeatedly using words like 'and', 'very', 'nice' and 'got'. All of them are very overworked. Change your sentence structure or find a synonym to replace them. Don't begin sentences with 'and', 'but' or 'also'.

Nothing is more monotonous than the repetition of the same sentence pattern. Vary it by changing the length of your sentences and by placing clauses and phrases in a different order. There is a variety of different sentence structures you can use. Look at the following examples:

1. The bride looked radiant. (One **main clause**.)

2. The match was cancelled because of the weather. (**Main clause** followed by **dependent** clause.)

3. Because of the weather, the match was cancelled. (**Dependent** clause followed by **main clause**.)

4. Peeping into the bedroom, she saw that her daughter was still asleep. (**Phrase** followed by **main clause**.)

5. The Crown Prince, who should have succeeded his father on the throne, was assassinated last week. (**Dependent clause** inserted in the middle of a **main clause**.)

6. I had a shower, put on my new evening dress, dabbed some perfume behind my ears, picked up my handbag and rushed downstairs. (List of **main clauses** with subject 'I' 'understood'.)

7. Julie was playing the piano, Mark was doing his homework, Colin was in the kitchen and Karen was reading her library book. (List of **main clauses** each with a different subject.)

These are just a few of the sentence variations you can use.

USING THE CHECKLIST

◆ Remember to use commas in the correct places when more than one clause is used.

◆ Always check your work.

◆ Avoid unnecessary repetition and tautologies.

◆ Check spellings of frequently misspelled words.

◆ Vary your sentence structure.

◆ Avoid the use of jargon.

◆ Clichés are frequently used phrases. Avoid them.

◆ A simile is a comparison using 'like' or 'as'.

◆ A metaphor is an implied comparison without the use of 'like' or 'as'.

◆ Personification gives human characteristics to things that are not human.

◆ Use similes and metaphors to 'colour' your language.

◆ Delete unnecessary words.

PRACTISING WHAT YOU'VE LEARNT

1. Correct the following:

(a) The school are hoping to raise enough money to build a new drama studio.

(b) He gave packages to both John and I.

(c) Me and June is going out.

(d) The cat licked it's whiskers while the dogs' ate there dinner.

(e) Her work was very excellent.

(f) He hasn't got no coat.

(g) She could of gone to London.

2. Stimulate your imagination by creating similes or metaphors to describe the following:

(a) The sun setting over the sea.

(b) Thick fog.

(c) An empty room.

(d) A worried woman.

See page 166 for suggested answers.

Part Two:
English in Action

8

Writing an Essay and a Short Story

RESEARCHING YOUR ESSAY

The title

If you are planning your own title, make sure you deal with only one aspect of a subject. Don't make the subject too broad. If you are given a title, make sure you fully understand it before starting work. Remember that the titles of some essays can cover several lines and more than one sentence.

Example: GCSE Literature question

> Lady Macbeth was a complex character who dominated her husband. With detailed reference to the text, show how she achieved her aims.

During both your preparatory work and the actual writing of the essay, it is essential that you refer frequently to the title so that you are not tempted to wander off the point.

Think about the following:

◆ What is the title asking you to do?

♦ Are there two parts to the question?

♦ What research do you need to do?

♦ What are the key words in the title?

Planning your research

The most obvious place to start your research is the library. Here you will find books on all topics classified by subject, magazines, newspapers and also archive material. Some of this may be on disk. Archive material is very useful if you wish to use 'primary sources' as they are called. These are original letters, diaries, books and periodicals. Librarians are usually very helpful so do ask if you are having difficulty finding something.

Visiting and interviewing

You may need to visit places and people to learn more about your topic. 'Experts' in their fields are usually very happy to be interviewed provided they are given plenty of notice. It is also courteous to write a thank-you note afterwards. Make sure your questions are relevant and you have written them down.

Making notes

Avoid copying down huge chunks of material. If you do, you might regurgitate it in your essay and be accused of **plagiarism** (passing someone else's work off as your own). It will always be obvious to the marker when the work is not yours. To safeguard against this always 'translate' the original into your own words. Of course, you are entitled to quote directly from the text but in this case you must put quotation marks around the quote and acknowledge its source. (See Chapter 4.)

Briefly write down the facts that you will need to use. If there are examples from a particular text that you may need, make a note of the book and the page number so that you can refer back to it. Use headings for your notes as this makes it easier when you start to write the essay.

Sometimes your essay will not need any research. Perhaps you are sitting an examination and therefore have all the facts in your head; it might be a personal experience piece or something that you have to work out for yourself. Whatever type of writing you are doing you *must* make notes first. Write down quickly all the things that come into your head relating to the title. Sentences are not important at the moment. Words or phrases are sufficient. It is important to get everything down before you forget it.

Making a bibliography

Remember to keep a record of the books you use as you are usually required to identify your sources. Write a list of the books you have used stating the title, author, publisher and publication date. This is called a **bibliography**.

Planning the work

After your note-taking, it is essential to plan your essay. Your notes do *not* constitute the plan. They have to be organised.

Paragraph 1
Introduction.

Paragraph 2
Show her opinion of Macbeth by her response to his letter.
Her cruel delight at the King's prospective visit.
Her domination of Macbeth when he enters.

Paragraph 3
She mocks Macbeth for his cowardice.
Shows herself to be without womanly feelings.
Forces him to do her will.
Berates him when he returns with the bloody knives.
Continues to mock him for his fear.

Paragraph 4
Banquet scene.
Reminds Macbeth of his duties.
Covers for him when he sees the ghost.
Berates him in private for his behaviour.

Paragraph 5
Summing up of ways she dominates.
She mocks him.
Her own actions.
Forces him to do her will.

Paragraph 6
Conclusion.

Fig. 1.   Essay Plan.

STRUCTURING YOUR ESSAY

Your work should be set out in **paragraphs** and each paragraph will deal with one topic (see Chapter 4). From your notes you must decide how you can group your points so that the essay will flow naturally from one paragraph to the next. How you arrange your plan is up to you but remember to keep to the point. Use evidence to support what you say and explain why your quotations or references are relevant.

Remember that you must have an **introductory paragraph** showing what you are intending to do in your essay. The main body of the essay follows. From your notes pick out the main points that you will use and organise them under paragraph **headings**. Remember that a paragraph deals with one main idea but you may be able to group several similar points together. The **concluding paragraph** sums up the essay and shows that you have completed what you set out to do.

Decide the best way to approach your essay. This will depend upon what type of essay you are writing.

◆ Is it going to be a piece of narrative told chronologically?

◆ Will it be a descriptive piece?

◆ Will you be expounding a theory and supporting it with your research?

◆ Will it be discursive? In this case both sides of an argument are used and you must write a balanced essay with evidence supporting both points of view.

Figure 1 is a suggested plan for the Lady Macbeth essay: 'Lady Macbeth was a complex character who dominated her husband. With detailed reference to the text, show how she achieved her aims.'

WRITING THE ESSAY

Having done your plan, you are now ready to start writing.

Make sure you keep to the point by referring frequently to the title. Always keep it in front of you as you write. Make sure that your essay flows naturally from one paragraph to the next.

The introduction

Your opening sentence is very important because it will either stimulate the reader to read on or put him off. It should be concise so the reader can understand what you are saying. You should aim to interest your reader from the beginning. Sometimes it is a good idea to start with a question – perhaps a controversial one. Look at the following two examples:

> Was Lady Macbeth a complex woman who dominated her husband?

> Did Lady Macbeth murder Duncan?

The first example leads the reader towards the discussion of the title. The second one would be more appropriate for a more philosophical discussion of the actual murder. Lady Macbeth did not actually stab Duncan but she definitely incited her husband to do so.

Bringing to a conclusion

In your final paragraph draw all the loose ends together and bring your essay to a logical conclusion. Make sure that you have already mentioned the points to which you are referring. Don't introduce new material in the last paragraph.

PLOTTING THE SHORT STORY

Although you will probably not need to do any research if you are writing a short story, it is still important to plan your work carefully.

Planning the work

Write down an outline of the main events of your story in chronological order. Then decide where the story is to begin and how it is to develop. Will the events lead to an inevitable conclusion or will you use the 'twist-in-the-tale' device? The unexpected ending can be very effective if well done.

There will not be room for any detailed description as everything that is written must move the story on. Your reader will want to know what happens next. In a short story there is no room for any unnecessary words so descriptions of people and places have to be by implication. There is no room for long 'flowery' passages of description ('purple prose').

Writing dialogue

Dialogue is important in the short story as it can be used to give information to the reader. (See Chapter 4 to learn how to set out dialogue.) It can also set the scene and help to create believable characters. Effective short stories often start with dialogue and this carries the reader straight into the story.

Creating believable characters

Try not to have more than four characters in your short story. Too many become confusing. Aim to give each one a distinctive way of speaking so that each can be easily recognisable. There will be no room for detailed descriptions of each so their characters should be established by what they say, how they behave and how the other characters react to them.

Finding a plot

A story is written to entertain and in your story there should be conflict of some kind. It could be between a parent and child, or between two neighbours. It could be a spiritual conflict within a single character. Should the heroine have an abortion or not? The plot should be simple and there should only be one. There is no room in a short story for a sub-plot. Plots are all around you. Your own experience or someone else's could be woven into a short story or you could modernise the plot of a fairy story or a legend.

Introducing the story

The start of a story is always important. The first sentence should grip the reader and carry him or her forward. Make him or her want to read on.

EDITING YOUR WORK

When you have completed the first draft of your essay or short story, check it carefully for errors and see if it can be 'tightened' by deleting words or changing your sentence construction. Remember to write in 'proper English'. Avoid totally any temptation to use colloquial or 'texting' language popular on mobile phones.

◆ Check your spelling.

◆ Check your punctuation.

◆ Is each paragraph indented the same amount of space?

◆ Have you begun your dialogue with a new paragraph?

◆ Have you kept to the same tense throughout? (Most essays and stories are written in the past tense.)

◆ In your short story have you kept to the same 'person' throughout? Is it written in the first or the third person? (See Chapter 1.)

◆ Have you used colloquial language?

◆ Before writing or typing your fair copy, look to see if you can replace any words with better ones. Make sure you haven't repeated words unnecessarily.

Checking the essay

◆ Keep to the point and keep the title in front of you at all times.

◆ Write notes in your own words. Don't copy from a book.

◆ Keep notes brief.

◆ Make a bibliography.

◆ Plan your work carefully.

- Structure your essay.

- Economise on words.

Checking the short story

- Avoid unnecessary description.

- Don't have too many characters.

- Keep the plot simple.

PRACTISING WHAT YOU'VE LEARNT

1. Plan an essay using the following title:

   'Holidays abroad are a waste of time and money.' Do you agree with this statement? Give your reasons.

2. Plan the outline and write the opening of a short story. Use your own title or one of the following:

   All that Glitters

   Full Circle

   The Box

Summarising and Reporting

WRITING A SUMMARY

Selecting the points

Whether you have to write a summary or précis for an exam or whether you need to summarise a report for convenience, it is essential that you first thoroughly understand the meaning of the passage. Jot down the main points – using your own words. It is then a good idea to put away the original material and write the piece in your own words.

Sometimes you might be asked to summarise a piece using a certain number of words. Often the length required is a third of the original passage. Make sure you are within a word or two of the number required. Summarising is an excellent way of training yourself to write concisely. There is no room for any unnecessary words. **Adjectives** and **adverbs** should be deleted. So should any examples or illustrations. Save those for use in a longer report.

The final summary should be a competent piece of prose in your own words. It should read well and should follow all the rules you have learnt in Part 1 of this book. Study the following example:

Passage to be summarised

> Napoleon and Josephine were married at a civil ceremony on 9 March 1796 after the bridegroom had kept his bride waiting for two hours. Josephine, who was thirty-two, was older than Napoleon and as her birth certificate was in Martinique, she conveniently took four years off her age. The bridegroom gallantly added a year to his so on the marriage certificate they both appeared as twenty-eight. No relations on either side were present and the Bonapartes, bitterly opposed to the marriage, pursued a vendetta against Josephine that lasted almost to the end of her life.
>
> Napoleon soon found that he could not dominate his new wife as he could his soldiers. On their wedding night, she refused to let him remove her little dog, Fortune, from her bed where he always slept. Later her husband ruefully wrote, 'I was told that I had the choice of sleeping in another bed or sharing that one with Fortune.' The dog made his mark in history by biting the General in the leg!
>
> The honeymoon was brief as two days after the wedding Napoleon left his new wife in Paris while he took up his post as Commander-in-Chief of the Army of Italy. From there he sent passionate love letters to her and she wrote back to him though not as frequently.
>
> (Approximately 200 words)

Summary

Napoleon married Josephine on 9 March 1796. Each gave false ages so they were both registered as twenty-eight. The Bonapartes hated Josephine and objected to the marriage. Napoleon soon found he could not dominate his new wife as he did his soldiers. Two days after the wedding he left his wife in Paris and went to Italy as Commander-in-Chief of the army. From there he sent her frequent love letters but she did not reply very often.

(Approximately 70 words – a third of the original passage)

COMPILING A REPORT

A report, like a summary, should be concise, but examples and illustrations may be necessary in order to clarify points in the main body of the report. Unlike an essay, a report needs headings for each section and sometimes it is useful to include a brief summary of the whole report after the title page. It is important to plan the report before you start to write it. Note down all the points you hope to include and then organise them into a logical order.

Preparing the title page

The title page should contain the title of the report in the centre of the page with the name of the person who has compiled it underneath. Below this is the date. This page should also show for whom the report was written. (See Figure 2.)

REPORT OF THE STATE OF ST BARNABAS'
CHURCH BUILDINGS

compiled by the Churchwardens

20 March 200X

To all members of the Parochial Church Council

Fig. 2. Title page of report.

Providing the contents table

A contents table follows the title page. This may not be necessary if the report is short. However, if it is a long report, it is useful to list the paragraph headings and the pages on which they appear.

Introduction
The Churchwardens were asked by the Parochial Church Council of St Barnabas' Church to look into the state of the church buildings as it was felt that they were deteriorating. With the help of experts, they have looked in detail at the 'plant' and have decided that the time has come for a complete renovation if the buildings are to continue in use.

Fig. 3. Introduction to report.

Summary

This report shows that St Barbabas' Church has fallen into a sad state of repair. The Churchwardens have consulted experts on various points and have dealt in detail with both the church itself and the adjoining church hall and facilities. As will be seen, there is a great deal that needs to be done if we are to continue to use the buildings. A number of recommendations follow the report which is to be circulated only among members of St Barnabas' PCC.

Fig. 4.   Summary of report.

Writing the introduction

In your introduction it is important to give the background to the report. You should explain who had asked for it, why it was written and what it is about. (See Figure 3.) Follow the Introduction with a brief summary of the Conclusions (see Figure 4).

Making the report

Make sure your report progresses logically from one point to the next. You have already planned it by noting all your points in the appropriate order so now write each paragraph in clear, concise prose. Use headings for each section and, unless the sections are very short, it is a good idea to start each section on a new page. This may be thought a waste of paper but it looks better and impresses the reader.

Coming to a conclusion

The report should be followed by your conclusion and a list

Recommendations from the Churchwardens to the PCC

The Churchwardens have looked closely at the needs of the building and ask the PCC to take note of the following recommendations:

1. Repair the guttering on the church roof.

2. Redecorate the church hall.

3. Replace worn carpet in church hall.

4. Renovate ladies' and gents' toilet facilities.

5. Replace pews in church building with chairs, and carpet the church throughout. This will cost a great deal of money. It is therefore recommended that the congregation be informed and asked to contribute to the cost. The following recommendations are also made.

   a. The collection on Sunday 23 June should be set aside for this purpose.

   b. Members of the congregation should be invited to contribute to the building fund on a regular basis.

   c. A day of prayer should be held on Saturday 22 June to pray that enough money will be given and pledged to allow us to continue using our buildings.

Fig. 5.   Recommendations from report.

of the relevant recommendations you would like the readers to consider. Make them definite not vague. (See Figure 5.)

CHECKING YOUR SUMMARY

◆ Make sure you understand the passage you are to summarise.

◆ Select the relevant points.

◆ Always write the summary in your own words.

◆ Write in clear, concise prose.

◆ Avoid unnecessary detail and examples.

◆ Keep to the correct number of words if told to do so.

CHECKING YOUR REPORT

◆ Plan your report so the points follow logically.

◆ Produce a title page.

◆ Use a contents table with page numbers.

◆ Write an introduction.

◆ Write a summary of the report.

◆ Use headings for each section.

◆ Write a conclusion including, if relevant, your recommendations.

PRACTISING WHAT YOU'VE LEARNT

1. Summarise the following passage in approximately 50 words.

   Josephine continued to entertain lavishly and spent a

fortune on her clothes. She changed three times a day and was said to buy six hundred dresses and a thousand pairs of gloves a year. It was hardly surprising her husband was constantly complaining about her extravagance. But on one occasion her vanity saved her life. She was late in leaving for the opera because she spent some time rearranging a shawl, a gift from Constantinople, around her shoulders.

Napoleon had already left in another carriage so Josephine's carriage was some distance behind when there was a loud explosion. Fortunately Napoleon's coach had already passed the danger spot but had Josephine been following as she should have been, she would certainly have been killed as many passers-by were. It was the second attempt on Napoleon's life and the audience at the opera cheered in relief as he took his seat.

2. You are a headteacher who has been asked by the governors to produce a report on the staffing position at your school. Produce a title page, an introduction and a summary of the report.

(See page 166 for suggested answer.)

Filling in Forms

Filling in forms is something we all have to do for all sorts of reasons. Some are straightforward. Others are more complicated. For whatever reason we have to fill in a form, it is important that it is legible and that all the information that is required is clearly set out. If it is difficult to type in the information, it is a good idea to print it so that the recipient can read it easily.

WORKING ONLINE

Today, much form filling can be done online although the forms will follow a similar pattern to the 'paper' ones.

PROVIDING THE BASIC INFORMATION

Doing market research

Market researchers who send out forms to a sample of people usually require you either to tick boxes or to answer specific questions. The only personal details they might require are your age bracket, your sex, your type of living accommodation, whether you are employed and your salary bracket. These are the easiest forms to fill in although they often look daunting at first because they sometimes consist of several pages. (See example in Figure 6.)

Do you own your house?

Do you have a mortgage?

How many people live in your house?

Are you aged 18–25? ❑ 26–40? ❑ 41–60? ❑ over 60? ❑

What type of work do you do?	Professional	❑
	Trade	❑
	Manual	❑
	Self-employed	❑
	Retired	❑

How often do you watch TV?	1–3 hours a day	❑
	4–5 hours a day	❑
	Over 5 hours a day	❑

Do you take a daily newspaper? ❑   If so which one?

How often do you visit your local library?

Frequently ❑   Rarely ❑   Never ❑

Fig. 6. Example of market research form.

Name:

Address:

Telephone number: Home: Work:

Mobile number: email:

Date of Birth: Nationality:

Fig. 7. Personal details on any form.

Providing personal details

Apart from forms used for market research which are usually anonymous, the first page of all other forms will usually consist of your personal details (see Figure 7).

COPING WITH A VARIETY OF FORMS

Dealing with the bank

Most of your business with the bank can now be dealth with online but the forms will be similar to 'paper' ones. Obviously, withdrawing money is not an option and when a signature is required, a visit to your bank is essential.

Most of us, at some time, have dealings with a bank. Bank forms are usually straightforward and unless you are opening an account (see Figure 8), the two important requirements are the sort code, shown at the top right-hand corner of your cheque, and your account number, which is at the bottom of the cheque.

Opening a mortgage account
The first section of the form will be the same as in Figure 8. The following questions will be as in Figure 9.

Setting up standing orders and direct debits
You have control over standing orders and alter the amount as necessary. A direct debit means you give the beneficiary the right to tell your bank to change the fee when there is an increase. The sort code you will find at the top right-hand corner of your cheque. (See Figure 10.)

Name:

Address:

Telephone number: Home: Work:

How long have you lived at this address?

Occupation: Professional ❑ Clerical ❑ Unskilled ❑

           Forces ❑   Self-employed ❑   Retired ❑

Name and address of present employer:

How long have you worked in your present post?

Facilities required:
Cheque guarantee card ❑   Multifunction card ❑

Overdraft ❑: Amount: Duration: Purpose:

Amount to be paid into account monthly:

Signature: Date:

Fig. 8. Form for opening a bank account.

Do you   – own you own home?   ❑
                        – rent?   ❑
                        – live with your parents?   ❑
                        – live in lodgings?   ❑

What is your total annual gross (before tax) income?

Do you pay tax in the UK?

Do you pay the higher rate of tax?

Have you ever been refused credit?

If 'yes' give details.

What is your monthly expenditure?

Insurance . . .	Council tax . . .	Heating . . .	Electricity . . .
Telephone . . .	Water . . .	TV licence . . .	Car insurance . . .
Car tax . . .	Car repairs . . .	Petrol . . .	Child care . . .
Food . . .	Clothes . . .	Entertainment . . .	Other . . .

Total monthly expenditure:

Reason for mortgage:
Buying first home ❑   Second home ❑   Moving ❑

Amount of mortgage required:

Signature: Date:

Fig. 9. Form for opening a mortgage account.

To _____ Bank

Address:

Sort code:

Please make payments from cheque account:
                          name:
                          number:

Please pay to   Bank name:
                          Address:
                          Sort code:

Creditor's account: name:
                          number:

The sum of: £

Amount in words:

Starting on:
and thereafter at weekly*/monthly*/quarterly*/yearly*
intervals until:
or until cancelled by me/us* in writing.

Signature: Date:

*Delete if not applicable

Fig. 10. Standing order form.

Name:

Address:

Phone number:

National Insurance Number:

Name and address of previous doctor:

Please tick if you wish to register a child under five with
the doctor. ❑

Fig. 11.   Patient registration form.

Dealing with the National Health Service

You will also have to fill in a form when dealing with
the National Health Service. Fortunately, the forms used
when registering with a doctor have recently been much
simplified. Your National Insurance Number is sometimes
required for these so make sure you keep it handy as it is
often needed for other purposes as well. (See Figure 11.) It
is unlikely that you would be able to register with a doctor
online as you need to take some form of identification with
you.

Filling in a claim form

Unfortunately claim forms have become a fact of life. There
are few of us who, at some time, have not had to fill in one.
Perhaps you've had a car accident, or been robbed, or an
appliance has been damaged or broken down.

Name and address of bank:

Sort code: Account number:

How long have you had an account there?

Which other cards do you hold?

Mastercard ❑   Barclaycard ❑   Visa ❑
American Express ❑   Other ❑

Do you wish a card also to be issued to other members
of your family?

If so, state name, address and date of birth:

Fig. 12. Application for a department store charge card.

Bride's name:

Groom's name:

Date of wedding:

Bought by:

Description of gift:

Message to be put on card:

Method of payment:

Credit card number: Date of expiry:

Fig. 13. Department store wedding gift list.

These forms will often require more than the basic details. If you have a car accident, the insurance company will need to know exactly what happened. You must put into practice the rules you have learnt and write a concise account of the accident, as in the following example:

Details of accident

It was about 10.30 am on Wednesday 3 July 200X. It was raining and I had stopped at the large roundabout at the end of Send High Street. I started to drive slowly forward and realised another car was coming from the right so I stopped again. The car behind me did not stop and crashed into the back of my car, damaging the lock on the boot and smashing both rear lights. The boot cannot now be opened.

Making purchases

Paying for goods by instalments has become a recognised way of life. 'Keeping up with the Joneses' has never been so true and we all wish for modern appliances to make our lives easier. Nowadays we do not have to pay a large amount at once. Credit cards and department charge cards are here to stay and most of us own at least one. But before one is issued, you have to fill out yet another form. As well as your personal details, you will also need to answer the questions set out in the example in Figure 12.

Using a wedding gift list

Some department stores hold wedding gift lists so that guests can order appropriate gifts and have them gift wrapped and sent straight to the bride with a message. (See Figure 13.)

Make of vehicle: Model: Engine size:
No. of doors:

Date of first registration: Registration number:

Value of vehicle: Current mileage:
Date of purchase:

Do you own the vehicle?

Is it kept in a garage?

It is a right-hand drive?

How long have you held a driving licence?
What type is it?

Are you the main driver?

If not, please give details of other drivers:

Have you or any other mentioned drivers been involved
in an accident or suffered loss in connection with any
vehicle during the past five years?

If 'yes', please give details:

Was a claim made?

Did the accident result in a conviction?

If 'yes', please give details:

Signature: Date:

Fig. 14.   Car insurance form.

Taking out insurance

We all have to have insurance of some kind. Many insurances are required by law. We have to have our car and our homes insured. Fortunately these forms are not too complicated and once the first insurance has been acquired, a renewal notice only is sent in succeeding years. As well as the normal personal details, you will have to fill in details about the car (see Figure 14).

Claiming benefit

Sadly, many people have to claim benefit and to do so, it is again necessary to fill in forms. These are quite detailed but read them carefully and if you find them difficult to complete, ask for help at your council or social security offices. If you are claiming housing benefit or council tax benefit, the council will want to know the following:

(a) Your personal details including date of birth and National Insurance Number. You must provide the same information for your partner if you have one.

(b) A list of children for whom you receive child benefit.

(c) Details of anyone else living in the same house.

(d) Details of your work and income including any other benefit you receive.

(e) Details of any savings you have. The council may also ask for proof of these.

(f) Details of the house in which you live.

Filing in the tax return

The tax return must be one of the most complicated forms to fill in. Fortunately the tax office provides us with a thick booklet of notes relating to specific questions. Do use this as it clarifies points that may be confusing. It is now possible to make your tax return online.

Read the form through first and delete with a single line the sections that do not apply to you. As the form is comprehensive and is used for all categories from the high to the low income bracket, much of it will only apply to certain sections of the community. If you can get rid of the sections that do not relate to you, the form will not look so daunting. If you are self-employed, make sure you fill in the relevant pamphlet the Inland Revenue will send you.

If you have problems, do consult your local tax office. They are usually very helpful.

Applying for a driving licence

Driving licences are now issued in the form of a plastic photocard and paper counterpart. Both must be presented when required.

Organising your photograph

You will require an up-to-date colour photo similar to a passport photo; it must be of good quality as it will be reduced and copied. To confirm it is a good likeness it must be signed on the back by a person of standing in the community: doctor, teacher, minister of religion, civil servant, police officer.

Confirming your identity

You must also send proof of identity in the form of current passport, birth certificate or adoption certificate. The originals must be sent. Copies are not acceptable.

Paying for the licence

The current cost in 2008 for a driving licence is:

Provisional licence	£50.00
Provisional licence to full licence	Free
Duplicate licence if lost or stolen	£17.50
Renewal of licence from age 70	Free
Exchanging EC/EEA or foreign licence	Free
Exchanging a paper licence for a photocard licence	£17.50
Change of name and/or address	Free
Renewal for medical reasons	Free

Filing in the form

Most of the information required on the form is standard but you will be required to answer a section about your health, both mental and physical. You will also be asked if you can read a car number plate at a distance of 67 feet.

Signing the form

The form must be signed legibly in *black* ink and the signature *must* be contained within the appropriate white box.

Applying for a visa

Some countries require UK citizens to obtain a visa before entering their countries and once again you will have to fill in a form. Some of these can now be done online. In fact the Indian High Commission requires all visa application forms to be completed online. However, if your trip has been organised by a travel company, you will probably have to complete a form for the company who will then put it online. The details that are required for a visa are slightly different from other forms. Your date and place of birth and your nationality are required. You will also need to enter the same for your parents.

Applying for job applications
Application forms will be discussed in Chapter 12.

Replying to an invitation
Wedding invitations, dinner invitations, invitations to formal banquets all require replies. On the bottom left of the invitation it will say 'RSVP to . . .'.

RSVP stands for '*Répondez, s'il vous plaît*' which is French for 'Reply please'. It *does* mean that. If you are asked to reply, do so because your host or hostess needs to know the numbers that can be expected. Courtesy suggests you should do so as soon as possible so that someone else can be invited if you are unable to accept. Remember to reply whether or not you are able to attend.

WRITING LEGIBLY
Writing legibly on a form you fill in is vital. Every form is important so make sure that the recipient of it does not have to spend time deciphering your scrawl! It is a good idea to print most of the answers. If you are required to write something, as in a car accident claim form, then remember to write legibly and concisely.

- Don't write the account of your accident straight on to the form.

- Write it out first and make sure it is clear and concise.

- Then copy it out neatly.

ASKING FOR HELP

Never be afraid to ask for help when filling in a form. Some forms can be confusing but the company will be dealing with them all the time and will be only too happy to help you. It is in their interests too. It is much better to explain something to someone than to have to request that a second form be done as the first one is incorrect.

Do take a few minutes before you fill in a form to read it carefully. This can save you time later on. Make sure you fully understand it *before* you start to fill it in. Of course, if you are doing it 'online', it is easy to delete errors.

WITNESSING THE SIGNATURE

Before your signature some forms put something like the following: 'I declare that to the best of my knowledge and belief the statements above are true and I have not withheld any relevant information.'

It is also likely that you may be required to have your signature witnessed. This means that you *must* let somebody *watch* you sign your name and then he or she should sign underneath to say your signature has been 'witnessed'.

CHECKING FOR ERRORS

- ◆ Always look through the form first and delete anything irrelevant.

- ◆ Write out any details in rough first.

◆ Write legibly.

◆ Ask for help.

PRACTISING WHAT YOU'VE LEARNT

1. You wish to make direct debit payments to the Electricity Board. Fill out the form on the previous page.

2. Write out the details of a car accident for your insurance company.

Writing Letters

In spite of telephones, faxes, e-mails and the Internet, it is unlikely that letters will ever become redundant. A personal letter shows that you are thinking of someone; a business letter is a permanent record that can be produced, if necessary, as evidence at a later date. Unless it is recorded, there is no record of what was said on the telephone and a business letter can be more detailed than fax messages or even e-mail. Longer letters *can* be transmitted by a facsimile machine (fax) but the quality of the reproduction is not as good as the original. Of course, you can print out e-mail letters and keep them.

USING E-MAIL

When sending a business letter by e-mail, it is not necessary to put in addresses as the e-mail addresses will automatically appear. If you *do* wish someone to reply by post or telephone, you could insert your details into the body of the e-mail. The endings would be the same as for printed or handwritten letters.

Giving a warning

Do remember that a business e-mail is *not* the same as one sent to a close friend. Do not use the 'texting' language that you use on a mobile phone.

7 The Mount
Guildford
Surrey
GU1 9BS
3 August 200x

Dear Joanna

Thank you so much for your last letter. I'm sorry I've taken so long to reply but life has been rather hectic here – as usual.

My mother moved into sheltered housing last week and we had to decide which of her things should be sold. Her new flat is delightful and the house manager is a charming lady. It is a great relief to have her near me now that she is getting older. Although she is over eighty, she is very independent and still looks after herself.

Tomorrow my sister is coming down from Bristol and we are going out for lunch. It's ages since I've seen her as she leads such a busy life. I must close now. I have to catch up with some more correspondence before I go to bed.

I'll write a longer letter next time
With best wishes
Louise

Fig. 15. Handwritten personal letter.

WRITING A PERSONAL LETTER

Using open punctuation

Open punctuation is usually used now for letters. This means that, apart from the main body of the letter, punctuation is kept to a minimum. There are **no commas** after lines of the address and **no full stops** after abbreviations. Your address should be placed at the top right-hand corner of the page. Each line of the address should be aligned. Don't slope them. The date is set underneath it with a line space above it. Use only the figure of the date:

24 May 200X

not

24th May 200X

Leave a line under the date and on the left-hand side of the page against an imaginary margin start your letter:

Dear Mary

There is no need for a comma after 'Mary'. If the letter is handwritten, indent your paragraphs starting with the first one under 'Dear Mary' which is *not* indented.

Your ending is up to you. The semi-formal ending is 'Yours sincerely' which is usually centred underneath the completed letter. You can also use 'With kind regards', 'With best wishes' or even 'With love'. Sign your name directly underneath the ending. See Figure 15 for an example of a handwritten personal letter.

Blocking your letter

If your letter is typed, do *not* indent. Use single spacing and leave a double space under each paragraph to separate it from the next one. This is called **blocking**. Do *not* **justify** (align) the right-hand margin.

The ending, 'Yours sincerely' or whatever you choose, is placed against the left 'margin' and you will, of course, sign your name underneath it. You may type your name underneath your signature if your letter has been typed. Do *not* print your name underneath a handwritten letter.

WRITING A FORMAL LETTER

The same rules apply as in a personal letter but this one will, if possible, be typed and there are other rules to observe (see Figure 16). Opposite your own address, put the reference number of the company to whom you are writing – if you have one. There should be one if you have already been corresponding with the firm.

Leave a line underneath the date and against the left-hand 'margin' write the name of the person to whom you are writing and underneath that, put his or her position. Then write the address in the usual way.

If you know the name, use it. If not, start with 'Dear Sir' or 'Dear Madam'. It is better not to use 'Dear Sir or Madam' as it suggests you have not done your homework. Your letter stands a better chance of reaching the right person if it is addressed personally. Make a phone call to the company to ask the name of the Director, Sales Manager or whoever it is you wish to contact.

ENDING THE LETTER

The ending for a formal letter is either 'Yours sincerely' or 'Yours faithfully'. 'Yours truly', which is the same as 'Yours faithfully', is rarely used today.

'Yours sincerely' is *always* used if you have written to someone *by name*. If you have started with 'Dear Sir' or 'Dear Madam', you must end with 'Yours faithfully'. Underneath 'Yours sincerely' or 'Yours faithfully' leave five line spaces and type in your name. If you are female, you can put your title after this in brackets:

June Brown (Mrs)

Susan Coombs (Miss)

Above your typed name sign your usual signature.

Sending an enclosure

If you have enclosed something with your letter, put 'enc.' at the bottom left-hand corner of your letter and follow this with the name of the document you have enclosed. If you are asking for information, *do* remember to enclose a stamped addressed envelope (SAE). You stand a much better chance of receiving a reply if you do so.

DRAFTING YOUR LETTER

As when writing an essay or short story, it is necessary to plan your formal letter so that the end product is the best

81 Queens Rd
Clevedon
Avon
BS23 9RT

16 May 200X

The Proprietor
The Angel Hotel
Mouse Lane
PRESTON
Lancs
PR1 6RA

Dear Sir

I have to spend a few days in Preston on business and I wish to book a single room at the Angel Hotel from 9 and 12 Sept 200X inclusive.

Please confirm that you have a room available and let me know your prices.

Yours faithfully

John Devin
enc. SAE

Fig. 16. Formal letter.

you can produce. Think carefully about what you want to say and for whom it is intended. Note down the points you wish to make, put them in order and write your first draft avoiding any unnecessary words or 'flowery' language.

Checking your first draft

◆ Don't use technical facts and figures unless you are sure your reader will understand them.

◆ Keep your paragraphs short.

◆ Don't use slang or jargon.

◆ Don't 'embroider' your facts. Keep them simple.

◆ Make sure you have a beginning, a middle and an end.

The continuation sheet

If your letter is longer than a page, use a plain sheet of paper of the same size and colour as the first. It should be plain and not headed notepaper. Under *no* circumstances write or type on the back of the first sheet.

Leave three spaces at the top of the new page. Then against the left-hand 'margin' type in '2'. Leaving a line space, write the date and, after another line, space put the name of the addressee. Leave three line spaces before continuing the letter.

Preparing the envelope

Set out the address on the envelope about half way down and about a third of the way across. It should be written exactly as it appears on your letter. The name of the town should always be written in capital letters. Don't forget to include the post code. (See Figure 17.)

Mr Clive Chambers
14 High Street
WORPLESDON
Surrey
GU21 5EA

Fig. 17. Addressed envelope.

Printing the envelope

You can, of course, print out your envelope on the computer. There is also a facility for printing out labels.

PRODUCING A VARIETY OF LETTERS

There are a number of different types of letters you may need to write and it is important that you find the right tone for each of them. You won't use the same tone when writing a letter of sympathy as you will when you are complaining about a faulty product or poor service. Always keep the following in mind:

22 Beech Grove
Grayshott
Hampshire
GL 23 5RZ

14 June 2CCX

Dear Mrs Clarke

I was so sorry to hear of the recent death of your husband. Please accept my deepest sympathy. I only met him a few times but I remember him as a very kind, sincere man who always thought of others before himself. He will be greatly missed.

Yours sincerely
Judith Soames

Fig. 18.   Handwritten letter of sympathy.

◆ Who is to read your letter?

◆ Why are you writing it?

◆ What result do you expect from it?

Writing a letter of sympathy

This could be a personal letter to someone you know well or it could be that someone you know only slightly has been bereaved. (See Figure 18.)

◆ Be sympathetic but not sentimental.

◆ Don't patronise.

◆ Don't overdo flattery of the deceased.

Requesting information

Whether you are asking for information about a place, a person or transport times, keep to the point. Don't include unnecessary details. List your requirements and *do* remember to enclose an SAE. (See Figure 19.)

Sending letters to newspapers and magazines

These should be addressed to the editor. Unless it is a very small publication or a local one, you can find out the name of the editor by looking in the latest edition of *The Writers' & Artists' Year Book* in your local library. If you wish to write to your local paper, phone to find out the name of the editor.

Don't make your letter too long as editors have little space and a short letter is more likely to be published. (See Figure 20.)

Writing letters of complaint

These are the most difficult letters to write. You must make sure you get your facts right. It is a good idea not to write the letter when you are angry. You may say things you will regret later. You should draft and redraft your letter until

12 Churchill Way
Maidstone
Kent
ME16 7OX

27 July 200X

The Curator
National Portrait Gallery
Trafalgar Square
LONDON
W1 8EA

Dear Sir

I have recently written an article about Lady Hester Stanhope for *Kent County Magazine* and the editor has asked me to supply a photograph. I believe you have one in the National Portait Gallery and I am writing to enquire if you would permit me to use it. Please let me know the fee you would charge.

Yours faithfully

Jane Lomax

enc. SAE

Fig. 19. Letter requesting a photograph.

16 Prior Court
Sea Road
Brighton
East Sussex
TN4D 1NP

23 July 20CX

Mrs Margaret Peters
The Editor
Brighton Clarion
Brighton
East Sussex

Dear Mrs Peters

I recently tripped over in the High Street and a young man came to my rescue. I wish to thank him for his kindness as he would not give me his name.

I am nearly eighty so was very grateful for his help. His kindness has restored my faith in the younger generation.

yours sincerely
Edith James

Fig. 20. Handwritten letter to a local newspaper.

30 Chertsey Road
Surbiton
Surrey
KT22 8EA

3 July 200X

The Chief Education Officer
County Hall
KINGSTON-ON-THAMES
Surrey
KT1 2RS

Dear Sir

My daughter Clare is due to start secondary school in September. We put down Cheyney High School as our first choice as it is the nearest one to our home but we were told the school was over-subscribed and she would have to go to Littlewick Manor which is ten miles away. It is not even on our bus route.

I am writing to appeal to you to act on Clare's behalf to enable her to be given a place at our nearby comprehensive school.

Yours faithfully

David Watts

Fig. 21.   Letter of complaint.

you are sure it conveys the facts and your feelings without being impolite or overbearing. (See Figure 21.)

Applying for a job
This will be covered in Chapter 12.

CHECKING YOUR WORK

◆ Use open punctuation for letters.

◆ If typing, block your letter.

◆ Omit addresses when using e-mail.

◆ Use 'Yours sincerely' if the name is used.

◆ Use 'Yours faithfully' if starting with 'Dear Sir' or 'Dear Madam'.

◆ Plan your letter carefully and then draft it.

◆ Don't include unnecessary detail.

◆ Don't use slang or jargon.

◆ Avoid 'texting' language in formal letters.

◆ Don't patronise your reader.

◆ Keep to the point.

◆ Don't write a letter of complaint when angry.

◆ Don't forget to enclose an SAE if writing for information.

PRACTISING WHAT YOU'VE LEARNT

1. Write a letter to a hotel asking for details of their facilities.

2. Write a letter of sympathy to a widow you know only slightly.

3. Write a letter of complaint to a shoe firm complaining about the poor quality of some expensive shoes you have just bought.

4. Write a letter to a woman's magazine telling a short anecdote about a small child.

(12)

Making Applications

APPLYING TO UNIVERSITY

During their final year of secondary schooling A-level students will start to think seriously about their future careers. Many of them will be applying to university.

Producing a 'Personal Statement'

Some students are now being asked to produce a personal statement as part of their application to university. This should be single spaced on one side of A4 paper. Two thirds of it should be about you, your qualifications and experiences and one third should give your reasons for studying a particular course. This should include the career you wish to follow as it will presumably be related to the course you hope to study. Part of this can be used when writing a 'profile' for your CV (see page 150). In both the personal statement and the profile you need to 'sell yourself'. However, while you shouldn't be too modest, it is important not to go 'over the top'.

APPLYING FOR A JOB

Because of the increase in the number of websites and the increasing popularity and ease of e-mail, applying for a job has changed over the past few years. Most employers will have a website and from this it is usually possible to receive the appropriate application pack. It is also possible to phone or to e-mail asking for information about a particular job and the 'pack' can then be sent to you.

If you decide to apply, you can fill in the application form online and you can send your CV and covering letter by e-mail.

PREPARING A CURRICULUM VITAE (CV)

It is still important to prepare a CV detailing your education, qualifications and career experience. This should be relevant and easily readable, and contain only the details that a prospective employer will need to know. He will be more interested in your achievements in your last job than in the first school you attended. Your degree is of more importance than your ten O Levels or GCSEs.

Filling in personal details

At the top of your CV you should put your full name and title, followed by your address and telephone number. Some employers will also want to know your date of birth, your marital status and your nationality so it might be worth including those. (See Figure 22.)

Your CV is a means of selling yourself and you must avoid the temptation to play down your skills and achievements. Your prospective employer will want to know whether you are suitable for the job for which you are applying. So make sure that you include details which highlight how suitable you would be for the post.

(Miss)	Jane Pauline Strong
	16 Ashcroft Lane
	Barking
	Essex
	RM23 8EA.
	Telephone number: (020) 8547 8192
Date of birth:	24 January 1981
Marital status:	Single
Nationality:	British

Fig. 22. CV: personal details.

Writing a profile

It is a good idea to write a brief profile of yourself at the beginning. It introduces you and you should mention any relevant skill, achievements and experience. It also serves to illustrate your personal attributes. This would be similar to the personal statement used when applying to university. It would be useful to have two profiles – one for a specific job and one which is more general. Look at the following two examples:

Specific profile – application for a position as an assistant in a Senior Citizens' Day Centre

A caring, adaptable individual who has worked with elderly people for several years. Has great patience and is willing to turn her hand to anything within reason.

This is relevant to the position that is being sought. The words 'caring', 'adaptable' and 'patience' are particularly appropriate.

General profile

> An articulate, forward-looking individual with great organisational ability and managerial skills. Has held a variety of jobs in middle management and is now looking for promotion. Ambitious and enthusiastic.

This profile could be used in more situations. Don't be modest when you write your profile but don't go 'over the top' and appear too good to be true.

Organising the CV

There is no right or wrong way to set out a CV. Remember that its aim is to sell yourself so you should arrange it so that the reader can easily find what he or she wants to know. *Don't* include irrelevant detail but *do* include skills that you have acquired and your achievements.

Including your education

Sometimes an employer wishes to know your educational background so it is worth including that. State briefly what schools and colleges you have attended, starting with the last one and giving dates.

Putting in your qualifications

If you do not have qualifications, miss out this section and concentrate on your skills and work experience however slight.

If you *are* loaded with qualifications, enter the most important ones first. It is not necessary to enter all the subjects you passed at GCSE or Advanced Level unless this is required. Follow the example below for style:

Qualifications

2005	Associate of the London Academy of Music and Dramatic Art (Teaching diploma)
2004	BA (Hons) English and Theatre Studies
2001	3 Advanced Levels (English, History, French)
1999	9 GCSEs (including Maths and English)

Under this section you could also include any recent training courses you have attended. Make sure they are relevant and don't include too many.

Listing your career details

Most employers will want to know what experience you have had so your work experience should be listed. Put your most recent job first and list your achievements and the skills you have developed. Go backwards and do the same with your other posts. If you have had a long career, it is not necessary to spend as much time on your first jobs.

If you are a school-leaver, you could list any holiday or Saturday jobs you have done. Again do remember to refer to the skills you have developed. (See Figure 23.)

Identifying the skills

There are a variety of skills and throughout our lives we are developing and sharpening them:

◆ verbal skills

◆ communication skills

◆ persuasive skills

Career History

Company	Position held	From	To
Elton's Shoe Store	Manager	June 2004–	
Wyborne's Shoe Mart	Assistant Manager	Jan. 1999–May 2004	
Debenham's	Sales Assistant	Jan. 1996–Dec. 1998	
Harvey's	Sales Assistant	Sept. 1993–Dec. 1995	

Current duties:
Overseeing a staff of five.
Dealing with the public.
Ordering stock.

Skills developed:
Developed communication skills.
Learnt to deal diplomatically with customers and sales representatives.
Developed tact and diplomacy when dealing with staff problems.
Developed creativity by designing window displays.

Achievements:
Won an award for the best designed Christmas window 2005.
Introduced a training scheme for new young sales assistants.
Increased the sales potential of the store by customer market research.

Fig. 23.   CV: career history.

◆ practical skills

◆ creative skills

◆ mathematical skills

◆ analytical skills

◆ organisational skills

◆ leadership skills.

Julie Coombs
14 Seneca Road
Chertsey
Surrey
KT21 6EA
Telephone: 01932 520034

Date of Birth: 24 November 1980   Marital status: single

Profile: A conscientious, hard-working individual who enjoys working with children, has great organisational ability and is very adaptable.

Education:	Bristol University	1999–2003
	St Peter's School, Walton	1991–1999
	Hogarth Primary School, Walton	1985–1991

Qualifications:	PGCE (Teaching Cert.)	2003
	BA (Hons 2.1) English	2002
	3 A Levels	1999
	9 GCSEs	1997

Career history: Teacher at Prior Court School, Weybridge 2003–present

Skills and achievements: In charge of school library for three months; developed organisational skills and patience. Helped direct two school plays and took a number of rehearsals. On pastoral committee and worked with disadvantaged children. Helped to set and organise junior examinations.

Leisure interests: Reading, listending to music, playing tennis.

Fig. 24. Example of a CV.

Including hobbies and interests

If you think it would be helpful, include a short section on your leisure time interests. This helps to give a 'rounded' picture of you and might show a prospective employer how you would fit into the firm. However, don't include too much in case your prospective employer thinks you will have no time for work!

Keep it short
Don't have your CV any longer than three pages and make it shorter if you can.

FILLING IN THE APPLICATION FORM

Some firms still issue application forms for jobs but your CV will nevertheless be useful as the forms are often very basic and there is not much room for the information. Having done your CV, you can always extract a section to include with your form.

Chapter 10 dealt with the filling in of other forms. The same rules apply to an application form. The completed form must be legible and all the information that is required must be provided. If the space is too small for your jobs or your qualifications, write in 'see attached sheet' and include the relevant sections of your CV. Most firms will be happy for you to send the form and CV by e-mail.

The form will require the same personal details as any other. Following that, there may be sections for your education, qualifications and experience (see Figure 25). At the end of

Application for position as:	Second in English Department
At:	The Barn School, Borden, Hants, GU35 0RZ
Name:	Julie Coombs Title: Miss
Address:	14 Seneca Road, Chertsey, Surrey, KT21 6EA
Telephone:	Home: 01932 520034 Work: 01932 564033
Date of birth:	24 November 1980
Education:	Bristol University 1999–2003 St Peter's School, Walton 1991–1999 Hogarth Primary School Walton 1985–1991
Qualifications:	PGCE (Teaching Cert.) 2003 BA (Hons 2.1) English 2002 3 A Levels (English, French, History) 1999 9 GCSEs (including English and Maths) 1997
Previous posts held:	Prior Court School, Weybridge 2003–present
Position:	Teaching English at all levels Assistant librarian

Fig. 25.   Application form.

the form there may be a blank section in which you are asked to add anything else you think might be relevant.

WRITING A COVERING LETTER

It is always a good idea to send a covering letter with both a CV and an application form. It will follow the same format as the formal letter in Chapter 11. When e-mailing, the addresses are unnecessary. The letter can give more details and also stress your interest in the job. Don't make it too long. One side of A4 or less should be sufficient. You should, of course, draft it out before you send the final letter. Highlight relevant points from your CV and say why you would like the position for which you are applying. (See Figure 26.)

ACQUIRING REFEREES

Referees are usually people of standing in the community – a doctor, a vicar, a teacher.

Teachers are often asked to be referees and they are usually willing. If you have just left school, one of your teachers and your headteacher would be useful referees. But do ask them first.

You should also ask your last employer to be a referee. This can be difficult if he does not know you are applying for another job. It is better to let him know as the new employer will certainly get in touch. If you are a school-leaver and you have had regular Saturday or evening employment, you could ask your current boss.

14 Seneca Road
Chertsey
Surrey
KT21 6EA

6 April 200X

Mr Keith Green
Headteacher
The Barn School
BORDEN
Hampshire GU35 0RZ

Dear Mr Green

I enclose an application form for the post of Second in the English Department at the Barn School.

For the past eight years I have been teaching in a comprehensive school of 1,200 pupils and have had experience teaching pupils of varying abilities from 11 to 18. During my time at Prior Court, I have been the assistant librarian and was in total charge while the librarian was on maternity leave.

Now I feel I am ready for more responsibility and therefore I should like to apply for the vacant post. If I were appointed, I would work hard and always do my best for the school and the pupils.

Yours sincerely

Julie Coombs

Fig. 26. Covering letter.

The names, addresses and status of your referees can be included on a separate sheet. It is not essential to include them when first applying for a job although it is sometimes useful for a prospective employer to have an immediate contact.

> Remember to check with your referees *before* submitting their names.

CHECKING FOR ERRORS

◆ Sell yourself.

◆ Prepare a striking profile.

◆ Use only relevant material in your CV.

◆ List education, qualifications and jobs in reverse order – most recent first.

◆ Remember to include your skills and achievements but don't overdo them.

◆ Always write legibly.

◆ Remember to *ask* before offering a referee's name.

PRACTISING WHAT YOU'VE LEARNT

1. Write two personal profiles – one for a specific job and one general one.

2. Plan your CV.

3. Write a covering letter to accompany your CV. Identify the post for which you are applying.

Suggested Answers

CHAPTER 1

1. Completing the sentences

(a) The harassed housewife rushed into the shop.
(b) Sarah ran across the road.
(c) Queen Victoria was not amused.
(d) Oxford University won the race.
(e) His cousin was very angry.
(f) He wanted to play tennis.
(g) The telephone was ringing.
(h) He worked on the computer.
(i) The castle was a ruin.
(j) The dog bit John.

2. Replacing nouns with pronouns

Sarah was working in her office. She looked out of the window and saw the window cleaner. The windows were very dirty. They needed cleaning. She asked him if he had rung the front door bell. He said he had. He asked if she wanted her windows cleaned. She said she did want them cleaned. He said the garden gate was unlocked. She was sure she had locked it. When the window cleaner rang the door bell for the second time, she heard it.

CHAPTER 2

1. Correcting sentences

(a) The Government is preparing to discuss the new Divorce Bill.
(b) That class is very noisy today.

(c) Everyone had done his (her) work.
(d) The crowd was enthusiastic.

2. Adding conjunctions or relative pronouns

Although it was so cold, Judith decided to play tennis at the club. Then she discovered that her tennis racquet, **which** was very old, had a broken string. **Because** there was no time to have it mended, she knew she would not be able to play **and** she angrily threw the racquet across the room. It knocked over a china figurine **which** broke in half. She started to cry. **When** the telephone rang, she rushed to answer it **but** it was a wrong number. She picked up the broken ornament. **If** she found some superglue, would she be able to mend it? **Before** she broke it, she had forgotten how much she liked it. **As** she had nothing better to do, she decided to go to the town to buy some glue. **While** she was shopping, she met Dave **who** invited her to a party that evening. She was thrilled **as** she had been feeling very depressed.

3. Adding phrases

(a) **Flinging open the door**, he hurtled into the room.
(b) He broke his leg **falling off his horse**.
(c) Mr Samson, **a tall, elegant man**, walked on to the stage.
(d) **Climbing into bed**, she thought about the events of the day.
(e) **Bouncing her ball**, the child giggled.

CHAPTER 3

1. Putting in the full stops

John was furious. He stormed out of the house slamming the door behind him. Never again would he try to help anyone. He'd gone to Peter to offer financial aid and Peter had angrily thrown his offer back in his face. Surely he could have shown some gratitude. Now he would be late for work and he had an early appointment with an important client.

2. Using commas

The sun shone down from a brilliant blue sky, the slight breeze ruffled the long grass, the scent of roses was all around and the birds were twittering happily in the trees. Emma, who had been feeling sad, suddenly felt more cheerful. The summer had come at last, hadn't it? While she wandered down the garden path, she thought about the letter she'd received that morning.

3. Using the semicolon, colon and dash

The team – those who were present – lined up to meet the new manager; they had had a bad season. Clive hoped Brian would improve their chances of promotion. At the moment the team was a disaster: the goalkeeper never saw the ball until it was too late, the defence players were too slow and the captain was indecisive.

4. Remembering the question mark and the exclamation mark

'I don't believe it!' she exclaimed.
'Why not?' he enquired.
Surely it could not be true. Why hadn't she been told before? It wasn't fair. Why was she always the last to hear anything? If she'd been the one going to New York, she'd probably only have heard about it after she should have left. Why had Pat been offered the chance of a lifetime? Hadn't she worked just as hard?

CHAPTER 4

1. Putting into indirect speech

John asked Susan if she would go to the dance. Susan replied that she couldn't because she was going to a wedding.

2. Play

Ruth: I've got so much to do.
Brian: The wedding's not for ages.
Ruth: But there's food to order, the wedding cake to make and the dresses to buy. (Starts to clear table)
Brian: (Goes to door) I have to go to the office today. I'll be back for dinner.
Ruth: Wait. I want you to do some shopping for me. I've got a list somewhere.

3. Punctuating dialogue

'Where were you at ten o'clock yesterday morning?' the policeman asked.

John thought for a moment and then said, 'I was shopping.'

'Where?'

'I can't remember.'

'Try to remember. It's important.'

John sighed and fidgeted. He wished his mother would come in. Perhaps he should offer the policeman a cup of tea.

'Would you like a drink?' he asked.

'Not while I'm on duty,' the policeman replied coldly.

CHAPTER 5

1. Forming plurals

ladies, companies, monkeys, tomatoes, boas, princesses, dances

2. Adding -ing

dining, living, hitting, hopping, skipping, writing, mating, mining

3. Forming adverbs

happily, joyfully, kindly, angrily, wonderfully, clearly, quickly, carelessly

4. Correcting the sentences

(a) I <u>know</u> you are <u>there</u>.

(b) I can <u>see two</u> ships on the <u>sea</u>.

(c) Did you <u>know their</u> house is <u>to</u> be sold?

(d) <u>Here</u> is <u>your</u> packed lunch.

(e) <u>There</u> is a <u>hole</u> in your jacket.

(f) You can go to London <u>too</u>.

(g) The teacher kept in the <u>whole</u> class.

(h) The violinist took a <u>bow</u>.

(i) Because of the wind, the <u>bough</u> of the tree broke.

(j) She <u>passed through</u> the crowd.

(k) He <u>threw</u> the ball.

(l) <u>No</u> milk was left today.

5. Completing the passage

There were no ships on the **sea** that morning. She could **see** the white foam as the waves crashed on the shore. She would **know** when **their** car arrived as it would drive **through** the gate. Idly, she **threw** a stone into the **sea**. The **boughs** of the trees on the cliff **were** swaying in the wind. It was **too** cold **to** sit still. Kicking off her sandals, she noticed she had **two** holes in her socks. She had intended to **wear** her new ones. Her hair ribbon had also come undone and crossly she tied it in a **bow** and stood up, holding her shoes. **Now** she could **hear** the car

6. Using initials

n.	noun
v.t.	verb transitive
v.i.	verb intransitive
a.	adjective
adv.	adverb

7. Making use of synonyms

It was a **sunny** day so the children decided to have a picnic. They **sauntered** along the cliff path and **clambered** down to the beach. The waves crashed on the shore as they ate their **delicious** lunch.

CHAPTER 6

1. Putting in apostrophes

Carefully he picked up John's bundle. It wasn't very heavy. He glanced warily at the cave's entrance. It was very dark. The picnic baskets still lay where they'd been thrown. He stepped into the cave and almost fell over a pile of little rubber tubes that looked like mice's tails. Inside there was a boulder of rock. Its smooth surface glistened like gold. John's hands shook. He wished he'd stayed with his brothers. His parents' quarrel had upset him and that was why he'd run away. In a week's time they were going on holiday. He wished now that he'd stayed at home as he'd been told.

2. Using abbreviations

The foll. doc. from Mrs Barker gives info. about the lectures to be given by Prof. Peter Coombs in Sept. and Oct. in St Margaret's Church Hall. The Hall is in Church Rd and is situated near the station. Prof. Peter Coombs will be accompanied by Dr Martin.

CHAPTER 7

1. Correcting the sentences

(a) The school **is** hoping to raise enough money to build a new drama studio.
(b) He gave packages to both John and **me**.
(c) **I** and June are going out.
(d) The cat licked **its** whiskers while the **dogs** ate their dinner.
(e) Her work was excellent.
(f) He hasn't got **a** coat.
　　He's got no coat.
(g) She could **have** gone to London.

CHAPTER 9

1. Writing a summary

Josephine spent a fortune on her clothes and Napoleon complained about her extravagance. But on one occasion her vanity saved her life. Because she had spent extra time arranging a new shawl around her shoulders, her carriage left late and she consequently missed the bomb that killed several bystanders. (Approx. 50 words)

Glossary

Acronym. A word formed from the initial letters of other words.

Adjective. A word that describes a noun.

Adverb. A word that qualifies a verb, an adjective or another adverb.

Articles. The a, an.

Bibliography. A list of books that have been used.

Clause, dependent. A group of words containing a verb that depends on the main clause. They cannot stand alone.

Clause, main. A group of words that contain both a subject and a verb and make sense by themselves.

Conjunction. A word that links two clauses together.

CV (Curriculum Vitae). A resumé of one's education, qualifications and jobs held.

Gerund. A present participle used as a noun.

Homonyms. Words that are spelt the same but have different meanings and are sometimes pronounced differently.

Homophones. Words that are pronounced the same but spelt differently and have different meanings.

Inverted commas. Speech marks: put around speech and quotations.

Jargon. Words or expressions used by a particular group of people.

Justify. Adjust margins so they are level.

Metaphor. An implied comparison of two things.

Noun, abstract. A word that denotes a quality or state.

Noun, collective. A singular word which refers to a group of people or things.

Noun, concrete. The name of a thing.

Noun, proper. The name of a person or place. It always begins with a capital letter.

Object. A **noun** or **pronoun** that follows the **verb** and is related to the **subject**.

Paragraph. A group of sentences dealing with the same topic.

Personify. Giving an inanimate object human characteristics.

Phrase. A group of words not necessarily containing a verb or making sense on its own.

Plagiarism. Using someone else's work as your own.

Preposition. A word that governs a noun or pronoun.

Pronoun, interrogative. A pronoun that is used at the start of a question.

Pronoun, personal. A word that takes the place of a noun.

Pronoun, relative. This has a similar role to a **conjunction**. It joins **clauses** together but is closely linked to a **noun.**

Prose. Written language in sentences and paragraphs.

Referee. Someone who is asked to give a reference to an employer.

Simile. A comparison of two things using 'like' or 'as'.

Subject. The **noun** or **pronoun** on which the rest of the **clause** depends.

Summary. A shortened version of a longer piece of writing.

Synonym. A word that can be used to replace another.

Tautology. A statement that is repeated in a different way in the same sentence.

Thesaurus. A book which will give a selection of synonyms.

Topic sentence. The main sentence in a paragraph. This is elaborated in the rest of the paragraph.

Verb, intransitive. A **verb** that is *not* followed by an **object**.

Verb, irregular. A verb that does not follow the usual pattern.

Verb, transitive. A **verb** that *is* followed by an **object**.

Further Reading

The King's English, Fowler, Oxford.

How To Pass Your Exams, Mike Evans (How To Books, 3rd edition, 2009)

How To Write an Assignment, Pauline Smith (How To Books, 7th edition, 2009).

Improve Your Punctuation and Grammar, Marion Field (How To Books, 3rd edition, 2009).

Quick Solutions to Common Errors in English, Angela Burt (How To Books, 4th edition, 2009).

Roget's Thesaurus, Longman.

Writing a Report, John Bowden (How To Books, 8th edition, 2008).

Writing an Essay, Brendan Hennessy (How To Books, 5th edition, 2008).

Index

Quick Solutions to Common Errors in English
An A-Z guide to spelling, punctuation and grammar
ANGELA BURT

'You will never doubt your written English again.'
– *Evening Standard*

'A straightforward and accessible handbook for anyone
who ever has a query about correct English – and that's all
of us.' – *Freelance News*

'This is an excellent book; good value and useful . . . buy it!'
– *V. Tilbury, Cranfield University*

ISBN 978-1-84528-361-2

Writing a Report
How to prepare, write and present effective reports
JOHN BOWDEN

'What is special about the text is that it is more than just
how to 'write reports'; it gives that extra really powerful
information that can, and often does, make a difference. It
is by far the most informative text covering report writing
that I have seen... This book would be a valuable resource
to any practising manager. ' – *Training Journal*

'With the help of this sensible step-by-step guide, anybody
can develop first-rate report writing skills.'
– *Building Engineer*

ISBN 978-1-84528-293-6

Model Everyday Letters
How to write and set out formal letters and documents
ANGELA BURT

'. . . from writing a formal acceptance of a wedding invitation, putting together a job application letter and saying the right thing in an absence note for a child who has been away from school . . . There are correct and incorrect ways of this kind of everyday writing, and Angela Burt shows just how it should be done.' – *Writers' News*

'. . . so helpful in guiding you through the formalities and principles.' – *Writing Magazine*

ISBN 978-1-84528-316-2

Improve Your Punctuation and Grammar
MARION FIELD

'Invaluable guide...after reading this book, you will never again find yourself using a comma instead of a semi-colon.'
– *Evening Standard*

'I can't recommend this book highly enough. Every writer should have a copy.' – *Writers' Bulletin*

ISBN 978-1-84528-329-2

How To Pass Your Exams
MIKE EVANS

'Brisk, shrewd and full of useful tips.' – *Daily Telegraph*

'If you want a book that is excellently written that will show you how to study and approach exams, buy this!' – Amazon Reader Review

Reading this book really will make a difference to exam performance, whatever exams you're taking – professional or academic, Master's level or GCSE and A level, essay or multiple choice.

ISBN 978-1-85703-323-0

How To Write Essays
DON SHIACH

'Guides to essay writing enter a crowded field but this one has the merit of being concise and clear and its advice plainly comes from someone with a lot of practical experience of teaching writing. As someone who teaches students to write essays I would have no hesitation in recommending this title. It is attractively written and laid out and it will be of immediate value to anyone who wants to master the art of essay-writing.' Amazon

ISBN 978-1-84528-341-4

Introduction to Research Methods
DR CATHERINE DAWSON

'I would certainly recommend this book to others. I found it extremely informative and will refer to it often.' A reader, UK

'It is compact, practical, easy to read and well laid out. If every student kept a copy by him/her during the course of the research, as a quick guide, it would certainly assist methodology and results.' – *Training Journal*

ISBN 978-1-84528-367-4

Read Faster, Recall More
Use proven techniques for speed reading and maximum recall
GORDON WAINWRIGHT

In today's information laden world, time is valuable. Reports, reference books, contracts, correspondence, newspapers, magazines and journals are just some of the things you might need to read and digest on a daily basis.

If you feel that the speed at which you read these items and the extent to which you are able to retain their information could be improved, then the use of the practical tips, proven techniques and numerous practise exercises in this book could help you to reach your potential. With the aid of this invaluable book, you can save time and achieve more.

'. . . will help you to reduce the time spent on reading and recalling information.' – *Evening Standard*

'. . . purely practical and aims to help you in the professional environment.' – *The Times*

'A worthwhile investment.' – *The Guardian*

ISBN 978-1-84528-162-5

Writing an Essay
BRENDAN HENNESSY

This lively and practical guide takes you through the whole process. With it you'll write essays of distinction every time.

'There's a lot of good sense in this book.' – *Times Educational Supplement*

'If you're a student, buy it.' – *Writer's Monthly*

ISBN 978-1-84528-249-3